The God Beyond Organized Religion

THE GOD
Beyond Organized Religion

Laurene Beth Bowers

WIPF & STOCK · Eugene, Oregon

THE GOD BEYOND ORGANIZED RELIGION

Copyright © 2016 Laurene Beth Bowers. All rights reserved. Except for brief quotations in critical publications or reviews, no part of this book may be reproduced in any manner without prior written permission from the publisher. Write: Permissions, Wipf and Stock Publishers, 199 W. 8th Ave., Suite 3, Eugene, OR 97401.

Wipf & Stock
An Imprint of Wipf and Stock Publishers
199 W. 8th Ave., Suite 3
Eugene, OR 97401

www.wipfandstock.com

ISBN 13: 978-1-4982-3213-5

Manufactured in the U.S.A. 12/29/2015

In loving memory of my best friend for forty years,

Elaine Michelle Valerio

("E.V." to me)

March 15, 1959–November 6, 2012

Contents

CHAPTER 1
My Inspiration to Search for an Alternative God | 1

CHAPTER 2
Moving Forward, Moving Somewhere: How We Will Search | 14

CHAPTER 3
Constructing a God-Concept: Transactional or Transformative? | 29

CHAPTER 4
The "Why" Inquiry: Exploring the Options of God's Power | 51

CHAPTER 5
The Essence of "Me" | 80

CHAPTER 6
Divine Intervention: How Does the God Beyond Organized Religion Act in the World? | 100

CHAPTER 7
The Purpose of Life, Death, and Dying | 114

CHAPTER 8
The Recycling of One's Organic Essence: The Afterlife | 127

CHAPTER 9
Reflections on the Search—The Whereabouts Question Revisited: Where Do We Go to Encounter God? | 137

CHAPTER 1

My Inspiration to Search for an Alternative God

My best friend and I would sit around the kitchen island on counter stools, drinking watermelon wine coolers while delving into intense philosophical conversations about the nature of god, who we are in relation to god and whether life has any grander purpose than hanging around talking about god. She read extensively in the areas of philosophy and world religions, dabbled in theological debates, was educated in law and employed as a nurse. Having been raised Catholic and feeling betrayed by the actions of authority figures she trusted as a child, she frequently expressed her disdain for everything reeking of the religious establishment. She didn't refer to herself as "spiritual but not religious," repelling labels that limited her freedom to imagine new possibilities and possessing no internal need to belong to a collective groupthink. At the end of the day, I suppose she believed in god or a god or something resembling a god; just not the god of organized religion.[1]

She loved to conjure up compelling theological arguments, often brilliantly composed and artistically formulated, derived late at night when she couldn't sleep in moments of semiconsciousness. These reflections were gleaned from the sacred ground of a hospital emergency room, where children are rushed to be saved from a mysterious force, nameless and unkind.

---

1. In this book, "organized religion" refers to any and all major world religions practiced through the structure and function of an organization.

The God Beyond Organized Religion

She described her medical interventions as a declaration of battle against this force, and when she lost, she felt defeated in her helplessness. She surmised that if these are the actions of a benevolent, caring deity, this god could not also be a god of justice. If CEO of the universe, he was doing a poor job managing the company and should be let go. If some cruel cosmic comedian, who delights in the suffering of parents who only want the best for their children, she didn't think he deserves the adoration of the masses.

In the midst of deconstructing conventional images of god held to be sacrosanct, she would ask me, "Do you believe any of this nonsense?" I knew her well enough to know she was posing the question with rhetorical diction; according to her deductions, the answer should be decisively articulated in the negative. Of course it was all nonsense. She knew me well enough to know I agreed with her. Still, the question asked, the question answered, was the way we danced together. That dance continually cultivated an emotional connection between us as best friends forever. We met at sixteen, when we both worked as dietary aides at the local hospital. During a snowstorm, we snuck into the nurses' old dormitory, invited everyone we knew for a huge party, got caught and almost got fired. To keep our jobs we had to clean the entire building from top to bottom (and someone had set off the fire extinguisher while running through the building chasing everyone else). Sometime between then and now, I became professor of philosophy and world religions at Quincy College.

I too was divorced from the god of organized religion. I can't recount when the decree became official, but it was shortly after I got kicked out of a doctor of theology program (ThD) in one of Boston's most prestigious educational institutions. Reason: failure to pass a comprehensive exam or at least by their standards, the inability (or unwillingness?) to adjust my thinking to conform to the dead theologians' society. To be informed that my theological orientation was out of alignment with the male European view held in the sixteenth century was a compliment to my sensibilities, even if the educational officials did not extend such feedback in a positive frame. As one embedded in academia and a collector of graduate degrees, being terminated might have exterminated any interest in pursuing an approach beyond traditional methodology. Instead, the experience catapulted me in search for alternative paths to explore innovative theological enterprises.

I landed, rather gracefully, on the path of atheism.[2] If there is only one god from which to choose, and *this one is it*, and I don't believe in

---

2. Technically speaking, I am neither an atheist nor an agnostic. I do not refer to

My Inspiration to Search for an Alternative God

this god, then I don't believe in god (by process of elimination). Atheism has its attractiveness for it allows one to authoritatively avow "there is no god" and be done with it. Atheists, however, slide down the same slippery slope as believers: certain there is a god (the believer) or certain there is no god (the atheist). Neither camp is willing to hold peace talks to understand the other's perspective.[3] Once one is certain about the existence/nonexistence of god, there seems to be little incentive for conversation; no room for rebuttal, no space for speculation. Had one of us concluded, "Hey, I am now certain what I believe about god and I will never think any differently," we would have hugged, said goodbye forever and gone home (although admittedly, we might have moved on to talk about new trends for interior design).

Certainty is a destination. When some are anxious about the search, they become eager to be right and tap the period key to finish the thought and quit the questioning. (A comma can expand upon the thought and grants syntactical permission to envision new avenues of a concept.) Some people have an internal (psychological) need to be certain, often as a desperate measure to safeguard their self-esteem. They tend to value content (answers) over process (how we arrive at what we believe) and freely associate the end product of "knowing" or being "in the know" as if an usher is seating them to the center-front row of a concert hall. They favor being spoon-fed answers so that they do not have to think for themselves. They simply don't like to search. Holy adventure into the unknown is perceived as a risky undertaking. So the familiar, no matter how tiresome, is a preferable location. If displaced by life's circumstances, they don't care how they get to a more comfortable place, as long as it is quick and effortless. Obstacles popping up along the way prompt them to whine "are we there yet?"

Her question sounded a trumpet awakening those who feel compelled to sacrifice their innate curiosity at the altar of allegiance to organized religion. As adherents line up at the front door waiting to get inside to put in their time so their god will arrange good things to happen to them, they

---

myself as such because I don't want to squeeze my thinking into one particular box. The god of organized religion probably doesn't like being contained in a box either. I am raising the question whether one can believe in god and not be an adherent of one particular religion. When someone asks me, "Do you believe in god?" I am likely to say, "Yes," but when they ask, "What religion are you?" I respond, "I am not a member of any religion."

3. They are afraid the other camp will try to convince them to come over to their side. The purpose of peace talks is to understand another's perspective, not to get them to change their mind.

The God Beyond Organized Religion

cleanse their foreheads with sacred water wiping off any trace of reflective awareness. The women wear stunning hats, individualized and unique, some with taffeta bows, others have flirty feathers. Men, upon entering the door, respectfully remove their hats and hold them in their hands. The women are adorned in necklaces, jewels glimmering with a bling when they catch the sunlight from just the right angle. Some wear earrings close to the lobe while others dangle graceful lines of silver that, when they turn demurely touch the cusp of the shoulder and without interference return to their previous position. They are dressed in long skirts flowing seamlessly to the ground and would drag if it were not for their high heels that keep the hem hovering to the adjusted height. They enjoy getting all dressed up because, for most, they have no other place in which such formal attire would be appropriate.

Once inside, listening in silence and passively participating is the position of protocol which constitutes the worship of the god of organized religion. Relevance to life on the outside is irrelevant (and thinking it should be is irreverent). One just sits there in total boredom waiting for the whole thing to come to a joyful-alleluia-ending so one can rise up and get the hell out of there. (No one seems to notice that their god also got bored and snuck out the back door.) In between the commercials, the music either appeals to the eighty-somethings, with its moaning meter and depressing dirge or to the thirty-somethings with a bouncy beat and rhythmic repetition. The eighty-somethings congregate in well-lit, airy space while the thirty-somethings prefer a dark theater-like ambiance. When I attend a worship service with the thirty-somethings and the lights go down and the band comes out and rocks, I am half expecting someone to pass me an illegal substance (though legal in some states for medicinal purposes) to enhance the experience.

A select few remain symbiotically attached to the functionality of organized religion: to do so enables them to remain on the straight and narrow and behave in accordance with its stated (and subliminal) rules. Most were born into a faith package in which the overarching statute dictates one should believe whatever one's family of origin believes and the family of origin should believe whatever their ancestors believed. Loyalty to one's ancestry is demonstrated through loyalty to one's religious organization. Loyalty is the heart in the body of obligation. It pumps out the adrenalin of allegiance. When asked, "Why do you attend a religious organization?" they say, "My parents make me." The processional of kicking and screaming

My Inspiration to Search for an Alternative God

teenagers being dragged into a religious building by parents who don't want to be there either but don't perceive they have a choice, paints a painful picture of the postmodern religious conundrum.

On the horizon, the freedom to choose one's religious preference (or no preference) is rising from the east, emerging as a bright light from the heavens above, while the cultural norm of obligation to support an organization as a symbolic gesture of family loyalty (as well as national patriotism), sets in the west. This paradigm shift/trending grants the individual consent to determine his or her religious affiliation. This decision is based on one's anticipation that a particular religious organization has something of substance to offer in the quest for self-enlightenment. In response to what that service might be, religious organizers are saying, "Huh?" In the yesteryear of mono-optional culture, they did not need to concern themselves with such trivialities as clearly advertising their purpose and marketing the value of their product to the public. Ignorant of the fifth discipline of organizational dynamics, organized religion has fallen from grace and on the way down hit the lifeline button in the hope that divine deliverance would save the day.

In reactive anxiety, religious organizers are attempting to intensify adherents' level of commitment to the organization.[4] Adherents who possess a predisposition toward obsessive-compulsive behaviors may actually become "addicted" to participating in the organization. They eat, pray, love with the same energy they invested in their drug of choice. The organization is only too happy to encourage (enable) such fanatical volunteerism as their attachment feeds its insatiable hunger. In exchange, adherents are made to feel special, above others, chosen for an extraordinary mission. All participants receive a voucher that can be cashed in at their time of death for a balcony view on a ship that sails nowhere. For those who have never felt worthy or included in anything deemed important, who suffer with self-esteem issues that desecrate their view of the world and everything in it, this entrance into elitism can be intoxicatingly seductive. For the organization to be worthy of such infatuated obesity, it must exude an aura of exclusivity which weeds out the untouchables and squirrels a secret code of surreptitious hush-hush.

Before adherent-wannabes are fettered into the flock of favoritism, they are required to register for the rush of indoctrination. These

---

4. Due to the decline in religious observance, there are fewer people to do the same amount of work to keep the organization in business.

requirements demand submission to emptying their minds of the clutter called critical thinking to free up space for conventional dogma and a set of guidelines for proper deeds. One is expected to unquestionably accept the time-honored teachings passed down through the generations, from the canon of creationism to the prophetic posturing of apocalyptic transitioning. Regardless of length of service or allegiance to the organization, adherents are viewed as inexperienced in the exercise of spirituality; blank canvases upon which to splatter paint so as to create art appealing only to the artist himself.[5] The more the organization thinks for the individual, the more dependent the individual becomes upon the organization. Diversity of perspective, which would divulge diametrically opposed opinion for democratic decision-making, is *not* a core value (nor a peripheral one). As long as all adherents believe the exact same things about life, god, themselves and others, everything will go along swimmingly.[6]

To reduce the risk that some will begin to contest and confront the instructional whiplash, religious organizers stoop low to sermonize about the evils that lurk while encountering other religions. They falsify what other religions believe (either intentionally to promote their own interests or unintentionally as a result of ignorance).[7] Inaccurate information is fed to facilitate the suppression of intense interest. Fear is the mechanism used to control the mindset of adherents and micromanage their behavior.[8] Those who unleash their chi of curiosity, who can no longer contain the desire to want to know so that they can understand where someone else is coming from, are shunned. Anyone daring to question or challenge the reigning wisdom may be exiled from the organization or reprimanded and given organizational service. Religious organizers prophesy about a time of judgment at the way station, when one's eternal whereabouts are (pre-) determined. Even the slightest inclination toward iniquitous inquiry crosses

---

5. Imaginative leanings, self-expression and creativity are suppressed in the service of conformity to a collective ideological worldview and give credence to a collection of sacred texts.

6. Given the constitutional separation of religion and state, no external authority monitors the system's mental models to plug up any leakage seeping from the container into its cultural context.

7. Today, doing research to find out what others believe has become super easy with the internet.

8. Some say guilt is the hook with which religious organizers cast for fish. Guilt, however, immobilizes people and suppresses their energy. Given that organized religion needs people to do things for them, instilling fear is like giving them just enough food to keep them compliant and still be able to work.

My Inspiration to Search for an Alternative God

the boundary of blasphemy and trespasses into treason. Those who dare to discover new territory are condemned to a place down under with less than ideal accommodations.[9]

Mythological stories narrate the wicked consequences awaiting those who are unable to curb their abiding inquisitiveness. Religious organizers rely on a metanarrative, passed down through oral tradition,[10] and embellished to be applicable to almost any situation. The main character, an antagonist, has been comically crafted wearing a red, tight-fitting suit, with horns protruding from his head and a pitchfork in hand, set against the background of fire and brimstone. Quite colorful and highly imaginative, he is one of the most recognizable but misunderstood figures in all of religious-dom. Allegedly, so the story goes, he had some kind of falling out with the big guy and was banished forever to be the manager of the manger of misery. His story might end up being your story and so if you "do this" or "don't do this" under the rules inscribed on the tablets of organized religion, this character could end up being your new best friend in the place you will end up for all eternity.[11]

Another scheme religious organizers use to foil adherent's fascination to learn something about other religions is to profess the party line that their religious beliefs are "right" and all other religious beliefs are "wrong." The paradox: the group's rightness is dependent upon another group's wrongness.[12] They are only right to the extent they can identify a wrong-group to serve as a point of comparison.[13] Religious organizers survey their

---

9. When entering the classroom to begin a course on world religions, students who have been subjected to this terror will hold their arms over their heads, in a protective gesture, afraid the ceiling will cave in upon them. I'm like, "What are you doing?" The believer who is badly informed about the religious beliefs and practices of other religions may surrender their ability to reality test such quantum entanglement. They are the ones for whom a course on world religions is truly a transformative experience.

10. Most of the well-known stories are not written in sacred scripture, even though most people think these imagery tales are well documented as a source of authority.

11. Depending on one's social location and current variable of vulnerability to suffering, the risk may be perceived as too great and not worth worrying about. While many among the middle class now scoff at such seemingly silly stories of hellish fortune, they fail to appreciate how some may go to extremes to ensure that the next life involves less suffering.

12. If they redirected their energy to helping others rather than trying to prove them wrong, it would be a better investment in the quest to improve their own critical thinking skills.

13. Sociology has shown that the geographically closer another group resides and is differentiated by specific cultural characteristics such as race/ethnicity or socioeconomic

The God Beyond Organized Religion

surroundings to locate an available target toward which they can point their twisted fingers and exclaim, "Look at those poor souls. They could not be more wrong!" Deductive reasoning concludes, "If you are wrong and I disagree with you, then I must be right," while inductive reasoning concludes, "I am right and you disagree with me so you must be the scum of the earth" (especially because my rightness makes me holier than thou). The direction of the argument doesn't much matter as long as I am right.

Being "right" makes one feel good. When life hasn't been all that affirming and one struggles with feeling worthy and adequate, a ticket to board the special train, the one in which waiters serve you dressed in black tie and make you feel on top of the world, like you are important and the world needs you, can be enticing.[14] Religious organizers play this game by making adherents feel as if they have achieved special status in the eyes of god. They talk about how god loves them more than others. God will punish their enemies and anyone out there who has ever mistreated them and not honored them with the respect and reverence they rightfully deserve. God will forgive them for any wrongdoings and they no longer have to feel guilty about their own past indiscretions (but will hold their enemies' feet to the fire). Those who are members of the right group will reap the rewards of that group: god will answer all their prayers and make them prosperous.

The generation and veneration of a groupthink based on "rightness" builds solidarity within the group; that is, being right becomes the unifying principle of privilege and prestige. The perception is that every individual in the group believes the exact same things about god, embraces the same concept of god, the same worldview and agrees on every social and political issue. Any hint of difference is asphyxiated because difference threatens the security of group-rightness. The group refrains from having a conversation regarding any subject matter (with the exception of who is going to pay for the electricity to keep the lights on) because conversation leads to an awareness of individual differences.[15] The closer the cultural similarities

---

circumstance, the more likely they are to be selected as a target of the group's projection. This is known as "contact theory."

14. Casino management knows how to manipulate this desire. For those willing to gamble a lot of money, they give free tickets to concerts and other red carpet treatments that make them feel like a "big spender."

15. It is not difference that divides us: it is the way we deal with difference.

My Inspiration to Search for an Alternative God

among individuals[16] the greater risk that the group will fall into this pattern of relatedness.[17]

From the outlook of the "right" group, the "wrong" group is not viewed as a composition of individual people with their own unique personalities and personal struggles but as one blob of exactly-the-same-adherents.[18] Painting a group with one brush stroke enables the right group to dehumanize the other, swinging slurs, bullying the bastards and in extreme cases, violently pouncing upon them.[19] By demonizing the "wrong" group, they create a rationale to idealize their own.[20] To think they are the cat's meow, they look next door and reckon, "Thank god we're not like them! They are a bunch of buffoons; we are a bunch of brilliants."[21] The idiosyncrasies they cannot see in their own group (or stomach), they can see with crystal-clear clarity in the wrong group.[22] Unleashing Pandora from the repression lockbox fuels antagonism and intense animosity toward others. Negative feelings toward their own group are not tolerated and that tension seeks an accessible outlet.

Religious organizations which practice one-blob thinking also tend to practice split-thinking (demonizing the other to idealize one's self). Split-thinking divides the world and everything in it into right or wrong, selfish or selfless, good or bad, kind or cruel. In religious terminology, individuals are either saved or doomed, "in" the organization or out, religious or

---

16. Such as sexual orientation, race, ethnic background, economic circumstance, ability, etc.

17. One of the best reasons to encourage ethnic diversity in a religious organization is because individuals learn how to deal with difference and not revert to singling out similarities. The greater cultural diversity in an organization, the less likely they are to idealize themselves and demonize others.

18. This too is a form of projection. What they cannot see in themselves, they can see in the other group. What they do not like about the other group is a projection from what they do not like about their own group.

19. Without difference of opinion or perspective, extremism is activated which can, on occasion, lead to a crusade of righteousness.

20. It becomes more important to be right and preserve one's status than to be respectful of the worth and dignity of another human being. No matter how wrong another person can possibly be, if only "wrong" in their choice of which group to join, they have the right to self-determination.

21. This thinking intensifies the group's sense of certainty and raises their esteem to the echelon of superiority.

22. It is irrelevant whether or not the wrong group possesses this trait or manifests this pattern of behavior.

spiritual. This enables the organization to preserve its self-proclamation of rightness so that adherents belong to the right religious organization.[23] The organization itself functions as the judge of who falls into which category because they know everything there is to know about their god and so can pass judgments on his behalf. All other religions worship false gods. Split-thinking infiltrates all perception and invades the individual's capacity for assessment (as a tool of critical thinking). It obliterates any hint of ambivalence, making "ambiguity" a swear word. According to the doctrine of dysfunction, there is no middle way.[24]

In some extreme cases, this antagonism toward the wrong group leads to overt violence. History chronicles a plethora of pillages, when those who were convinced of their rightness made it their mission to pound their rightness into others. Believing their rightness to be divinely inspired, they band together for battle to take on the platoon of badness (wrongness which seems to taunt). Perceiving the other to be making a mockery of their sacred commission gives good reason for any reactionary brutality toward the wrong group. They regard their weapons of war as "instruments of god." Their violent acts may range from subtle innuendoes to pulverizing entire populations via inquisitional conquests. Rightness, as defined by the dominant group, always prevails over wrong.[25] Not coincidentally, the wrong group often represents a group among the marginalized. The road to rightness is paved with comparative sticks and stones that hurt like hell.

The "right" group possesses an object that few (if any) other groups possess: the truth. Being in possession of the truth justifies their actions toward others. Still, what makes them super-superior is that the supreme god, the grand poohbah, the deity above all deities, bestowed *their leader* with the truth, imparted the penetration of proverbs and revealed otherworldly secrets. God could have bequeathed such divine wisdom to another group but this particular leader was chosen by him to receive all knowledge and

23. They also contribute to this thinking by having criteria for membership and threatening excommunication. The adherent is either in or out.

24. It doesn't occur to anyone that each religion may contain some truth or that each religion's truth is their own version of the truth. It is possible there are multiple truths preserving and protecting the diversity by which the universe was designed.

25. I refrain from naming one or two examples because most readers will be able to think of a few without my help. To name one or two may be at the expense of minimizing the violence that another group experienced (by not naming them) so that two groups have to fight for "who was/is the most abused by another religious group" status. Suffice to say, there has been so much bloodshed because one religious group assumed being right afforded them the right to hoard power over others.

My Inspiration to Search for an Alternative God

then to dispense it among those whom the leader deems laudable of such import. They are worthier than others and therefore will be prosperous, while the poor peons in the wrong group will perish penniless. If the group was already formed, they were nothing until he woke up one day and realized that he had been given the truth. How lucky they are to have such a leader!

Dispensers of the truth tend to be attractive, buff, male[26] leaders, preferably in their late thirties to early forties, with pretty wives who paint their faces to look pretty. Her reason-for-existence is to model the utter joy of being close to the dispenser. Everyone clandestinely wishes they were as close to the dispenser as she. Power pervades his being, not unlike the god worshipped by the organization. The distinction between him and the god is psychologically indistinguishable. He has a halo of holiness, an aura of awesomeness. He radiates power; all desire to be invited into his inner circle to participate in that power. In high school, he wasn't very popular but he coveted a wish to be so. Now that he knows everyone adores him, he doesn't know how to handle this reverence, leaving his adherents vulnerable to his whims. Boundaries become blurred and he cannot differentiate his own emotional needs from those of his adherents. He immerses himself in acts of charity which convince the masses of his well-meaning intentionality buying him a longitudinal latitude of indiscretion. He is adept at figuring out what people are looking for from a religious organization and manipulating the masses to meet his mega-needs.

Adherents soak up his truth like a sponge, sucking up every drop of water through a straw as if the river is about to run dry. His interpretation of truth is illustrated through his story of finding the god of organized religion (or more commonly the god finding him face down in the gutter). The worse he behaved the better because the gap between then and now testifies to how far he has come. They are impressed by his ability to turn his life around and find hope for themselves in their own predicament by identifying with his story: if he can do it, they can too. With charismatic magnetism, mixed with a high quotient of emotional intelligence, adherents perceive that he knows where they're coming from. Their identification with his struggle/story is the superglue by which they become stuck. As a result, he can say just about anything about anyone with a finesse of

---

26. While I am well aware there are a significant number of women who are clergy in almost all world religions, I am speaking here of the newer organizations which are often served by men who have no formal seminary education.

self-righteous indignation, tainted with a pinch of condemnation. On behalf of the god, he gets to discriminate whom the god loves from whom the god hates. Not surprisingly, the god loves everyone who is an adherent of his organization and hates anyone associated with another, especially those whose liberal leanings advocate for equality.

He denounces all who are born with a different orientation than him (he was cast from the standard model) and frequently uses words such as "evil," "sinful" and "abomination." His preaching makes the more insightful individuals wonder if his constant urging to control impulses is not his own uncontained, unconscious libido fizzing to the surface.[27] He receives much pleasure in the recurring theme that others are to be pitied and frowned upon as among the damned and doomed.[28] The pulpit of preaching elevates him to the pedestal of prerogative because everyone (literally) has to look up to him. After all, he is conducting a kingdom campaign (not sure what that is, but apparently it's a big deal). He is successful when, following the worship of their god, his adherents pull out of the organization's parking lot in their SUVs, and continue to feel "above" everyone else who are driving those low-to-the-ground environmentally responsible economy cars.

Unlike a restaurant, there is no menu when one sits down in a religious organization. They are serving one meal, one meat and if one is a vegetarian or vegan, forget it. Consumers come back week after week to chew on a package of regurgitated cuisine, exquisitely prepared to produce insomnia or a semiconscious state of acquiescence and cognitive dissonance. Adherents do not carefully inspect what they are eating and no one particularly cares if it's organic or contaminated with all sorts of toxins (used to promote quantitative growth). If everyone else is eating it, it can't be all that bad. No one stops chomping long enough to ask, "Does this food enhance my body's ability to be strong for life's challenges and compassionate to the challenges of others?" Just because something tastes delicious doesn't mean it's good for you. By the time one has swallowed that which has been dished out, the process of digestion has catfished their taste buds. I prefer to dine at the cafeteria of choice on an eclectic entrée.[29]

---

27. That which we obsess about reveals an intrapsychic struggle.

28. No one stands up and objects to his ranting and raving because it is not allowed in the organization's policy manual on worship etiquette. To arise from a position of subservience and voice, "I object," would be considered bad form and risks being escorted from the sacred space by the worship bouncers. (Every religious organization has them. They stand in the back of the worship space to make sure everyone is well behaved.)

29. I will be picking and choosing aspects of different religions in the attempt to

My Inspiration to Search for an Alternative God

How do intelligent, well-intentioned, caring, emotionally stable, mentally healthy people get hooked? Understandably, those who have recently experienced a major life-changing event, such as the loss of a job or relationship, the death of a friend or family member may be feeling despondent, desperate and depressed. They know their lives will never be the same and they seek a way to invent and initiate their "new normal." Such events are irreversible: you can't go back to the "old normal." There is no point of return. A group that offers emotional support and a periodic visit from the self-esteem fairy can be alluring as a quick fix to make one feel better in the short term. Any opportunity to alleviate suffering and diminish the impact of the disaster on daily functioning is an attractive alternative. Drowning in a sea of sadness, who of us would not latch onto a life preserver thrown overboard by an organization seemingly in ship-shape?

While nestled in our beach chairs by the ocean in North Hampton, New Hampshire, soaking in the sun, ferreting our feet in the sand, and once again drinking watermelon wine coolers, I blurted out for the first time, "I'm thinking about writing a book titled *The God Beyond Organized Religion*." After a poignant pause, a slight silence in reflective response, she lifted her sunglasses to make eye contact. "Do you think we can find this god?" I could hear the exhilaration in her voice: the thrill of the chase as her thoughts raced ahead. She loved the process; the dance of discernment. Driving over the sand dunes in her jeep, our hair blowing in the wind, the music blasting at full volume, yet barely audible, we were on our way to find another god, a god beyond organized religion. I just had no idea at the time that I would be making the journey without her. The demonic carrier of cancer had been hiding out in her pancreas wreaking havoc on her health. She died five weeks later.

---

construct an alternative concept of god. I have no investment in subscribing to one particular religion and overlooking something from another which may be beneficial to the search.

CHAPTER 2

Moving Forward, Moving Somewhere
How We Will Search

Last September, I got a text from her that read, "I have some bad news. Call me." She had just returned from the doctor who was concerned that perhaps, maybe, quite possibly, she had pancreatic cancer. I imagine the scene as she sits in the medical office, staring intently at the shiny white tiles on the floor with little speckled gray dots, as the doctor reviews her record looking for any sign of hope that the fatal facts could be false. The doctor shakes her head and says, "I'm sorry. You have cancer and it is pancreatic cancer which is the worst type of cancer because it doesn't respond to chemotherapy as well as some of the others." Dazed as if in a bad dream from which one cannot awaken oneself, she asks, "How long do I have to live?" The doctor, whose head is now feeling so heavy she too is looking down at the same tiles on the floor, lifts her head to make eye contact and responds (heavy sigh), "A few months." I don't know how the scene ends. I can't go there.

How does one move forward? What does one think about on the way home? What role has the god played in all of this? Does god make people get cancer? Is it to punish them for something they did or didn't do? Why does one person get cancer and survive for years in remission while another person gets cancer and doesn't live any longer than five weeks? How does one "make sense" of a situation that defies logic? How does one make peace with the angel of death, knowing her arrival is imminent even if one is resistant to her mission? How do I go about constructing a different concept of god beyond organized religion? How will doing so help me integrate this experience into my current reality? Which "ologies" will help me to move in new directions to discover new ways of thinking about god and ourselves in relation to god?

She kept repeating that she would fight against the cancer with everything that was within her. But when courage crept no further, she expressed feeling "scared." I don't ever remember hearing her use that word before and so it tapped a sensitivity key; expressing such an intimate emotion seemed like shining a laser light on a shadowy space within. She was feeling like a dog in a pit, pitted against another dog named pancreatic cancer. This dog is ruthless and relentless. She is the chihuahua cowering in the corner sensing something very bad about the situation and wondering why her owner isn't there to lift her from impending danger. What kind of an unsympathetic, uncaring god would not reach down from the heavens and rescue this poor dog shaking from head to toe?[1] Had the god put her in the pit to fight with pancreatic cancer? Was this a bet with another god or worse, some kind of perverse heavenly entertainment?

I didn't know what to say. I didn't want to say the wrong thing. I didn't want to add to her agony. I didn't reach into my purse to pull out one of those pithy religious phrases to alleviate my own anxiety.[2] Instead, I listened and responded, "I don't know what to say. I wish there was something I could say that could make all this go away." I tried to monitor my anxiety by not needing to fill in the seemingly endless silent pauses. I tried to imagine what it was like to be her, to walk on the path she walked, to be able to anticipate what kind of support she might need. I felt her helplessness, fear and bewilderment. And when there are no more words to express how one is feeling, I relied on the gift of catharsis with which we are created. I began to cry. We cried together. After an exchange of "I love you" and "I love you too," there was nothing more to say.

After the devastating diagnosis, she didn't want anyone to see her. Her mother, sister-in-law and a nursing friend took turns attending to her medical complications and giving her emotional support. Living seven hours away at the time, I had offered to return to my homestead community and help out in the rotation, but when I announced my plan to her, she was adamant that she didn't want me to carry it out. Feeling guilty and relieved

---

1. Knowing when to rescue and when to equip so we can rescue ourselves would be indicative of a god beyond organized religion.

2. For example, "There must be a good reason for this."

The God Beyond Organized Religion

at the same time, being excluded from the nursing duties worked for me because I can't stand the sight of blood and besides, I didn't know if I could watch her fade away. I suppose like anything else one doesn't think one can handle, I might have been able to suck it up and do it anyway. As the cancer ran its course and assaulted her attractive features, I knew she would not want too many people (including me) to see her in this condition. She never left the house (even to run to the store for coffee cream) without makeup and took pride in her appearance.[3]

I tried to text her every day. (I confess I wasn't always faithful about doing this.) On occasion, we would talk on the phone and I imagined her on the other end, sitting in her Jacuzzi in the backyard, drinking a watermelon wine cooler. But that image would be shattered as I became increasingly aware of how absorbed she seemed to be by actual aches; she would take stock of which body part produced what kind of pain, without acknowledging its etiological link. Each conversation became more focused on the distress of her discomfort, from the side effects of the medication to the excruciating abdominal stabbing which she described like a sharp knife piercing through her organs. I had never known her to be so internally centered. She was being physically tortured and that torment was all she could think about and nothing else. Still, not once did I ever visualize her lying in bed dying. I don't know why I didn't and looking back now, I realize I was in denial.[4]

I was at work one day, sitting in the office at the computer, daydreaming and not getting much work done and my mind wandered to wondering what others might be doing and so I checked Facebook. On my news feed, I noted people were posting RIPs on her page, over and over again and saying nice things about her as if she were dead. Hmm, what does RIP stand for? Is that an acronym for something? I tried to think about that for a moment but no answer was forthcoming to my consciousness. I felt confused and sought to remain in that safe state. Mesmerized, I kept watching the postings pop up on the computer screen. I decided to close the site and go back to what I was working on. A few minutes later, I thought about the RIPs again. Why would her nursing friends be posting these comments?

---

3. If it was important to her for me to remember her the way she was before she got cancer, then I intend to honor her wish.

4. I admit this is more of an excuse than an explanation: I could see her self-centeredness but not my own. The problem with being in denial is that it makes us self-absorbed and can be an obstacle to developing empathy for others.

Why would they do that? At the time, it didn't make any sense to me or at least, any sense that I could grasp.

Something within me felt this sudden, intense impulse to change locations. I wanted to run like hell in the opposite direction to avoid the oncoming train headed down the tracks. The next few moments are a blur on the odometer of reality. I collected my belongings, mumbled something incoherent to my secretary about a summons to get somewhere fast, walked to my car, opened the door, sat in the seat, pushed the key igniting the motor and pulled out of the parking lot. Thoughts entered my head while driving but I tried to exorcise them by turning on the radio. The music annoyed me: it seemed like the singer was oblivious to the fact that something tragic had just happened. I turned off the radio and made every attempt to keep the car between the white lines. Repeatedly, I instructed myself, "Don't think about it." I could do all the thinking about it I had to once I arrived home. All I wanted was to feel safely secure in the privacy of my protective surroundings.

Arriving home did not make me feel that much better, as anticipated and assured. I put my things down, let the dogs out, and began walking around the house, looking, yet again, for a location that would change the way I was feeling. From room to room, chair to couch, hardwood to carpet, nothing provided comfort. I began cleaning the kitchen (in one's moment of helplessness one can always do housework) but after awhile, to continue to do so, felt like a waste of a limited supply of energy. I don't know why I climbed into bed but I began to feel so histrionically heavy that I didn't think my legs could carry the extra weight, especially since my existential core seemed to have slipped from my heart into my gut. The bed appeared as if the consoling arms of a compassionate god which would coddle me. As I lie down and shut my eyes, sleep supplies some respite from reality. When I awake, it will dawn upon me that this was nothing more than a bad nightmare. She was not really dead.

Reality is a strong drink that must be sipped slowly. I probably fell asleep for awhile, and then my eyes opened, and after a few seconds of transitioning from one level of consciousness to another, the excruciatingly painful reality of her death interjected itself into my waking state: did this really happen? Is she really gone? My mind cannot manage such upsetting data. I need to let reality seep into my thinking in drips and drabs, administered intravenously in cautiously monitored intervals. It doesn't feel real. It feels like this is happening to someone else. I feel like I have entered another zone; another dimension. This cannot be happening to me. Make it stop. Make it go away. Help, I am suffocating. I can't breathe. I am drowning and I kick my legs trying to rise above the waves and grasp a gasp of resuscitating air. In the midst of my meltdown, I realize that she is no longer breathing. It's over. Pass the tea and sympathy.

When I awoke, I wasn't quite sure what to do. I again frantically moved from room to room trying to decide my next plan of action, teetering on how much reality I could absorb and hoping to find the room marked denial, that place of seeming security which offers a false sense of comfort, but comfort nevertheless. Once I found that room, it denied me access and as I tugged and pulled on the knob, pounding my fist on the door, "Let me in," it occurred to me I should find out if it's really true. So I looked up her mother's phone number, recognizing the number as the same one I used to call when she was still living at home. A voice answered, it was her sister-in-law who put her hand over the phone (I could still hear) and asked her mother if she wanted to speak to me. Yes, she did. When she answered the phone and said, "Hello," I knew her daughter was dead. It seemed silly to even think about asking. I had known what RIP meant all along.

In the days following her death, I went about my regular routine as if nothing extraordinary had been interjected into the everyday. No big deal, I reassured myself, people get sick and die. Life goes on. No one lives forever. Dying is just a natural part of life. I'll get over it; the experience doesn't have to be earth-shattering, just a hiccup of happenstance. A few moments later, I would think of something I wanted to tell her and as I reached for my phone to send a text, that pesky and piercing reality would raise its grotesque and gruesome head to remind me of its immanence. I put my phone back in my purse. Then the tsunami hit the unsuspecting coast with a wave scooping up everyone and everything in its wake. Something within me got caught up in the momentum and I surrendered to the tidal gods: *she is gone and she is never coming back*. How do I go with the flow of that actuality?

I went through a wake of wondering, "Where is she?" I realize this sounds like an ostensibly odd question, especially in light of the present reality that she was definitively deceased, not coming back, gone forever and ever reaching into eternity. It's not like she took an extended vacation or moved to another part of the country and while I miss her, she will eventually return home. It's not like we had a disagreement which conjured up hurt feelings and when those feelings subside and we feel a twinge of regret, both of us will want to reconcile. Occasionally, I still click on her

Facebook page, but it feels a little eerie to see her picture pop up as if she is still out there, somewhere in cyber space. I don't know why I do this, maybe I wonder if she has posted any updates concerning her status or whereabouts. There are a couple of new posts but they are by her friends who ran or walked a long way in her memory to raise money for a charity. I explore every avenue which may give me a clue about where she is and how she is doing; any sign of some reassurance that whatever her present location, she is OK.

One night at a party, I bounced the question off a good friend who knew her well. "Where do you think she is?" Looking rather dismayed, he retorted, "She's dead." I sarcastically smiled and demurely replied, "I am fully aware of that realism, but where did she go after she died?" He shrugged his shoulders, and leaned his whole body against the granite kitchen counters for support, buying some time to think of something that might sound profound and perfunctory, and when nothing came to mind, reverted to the traditional tagline, "She is in heaven with god." He appeared quite pleased with his answer. When I asked him where heaven is, he pointed upward toward the sky. The standard riposte, the unanswerable answer, the conventional comeback by those who had not given the whole matter much musing, only magnified the mystery for me. I set out on a meditative mission to pinpoint her present position.

I could board the Lockheed 5b Vega and fly to the remotest corner of the earth and she would not be there. I could travel to the four corners of the cosmos, and not see her face-to-face. I could return to every place we had ever trekked together, and not catch a fleeting glimpse of her. She is not strolling on the shore of some exotic beach wearing a bikini. She is not at work taking care of her patients with a stethoscope hanging from her neck. She is not at home stretched out on her black leather couch watching her flat widescreen television. She is not here and she is not over there. Only a little while ago, she was in all of these places. I don't get it. It doesn't make logical sense to me. I just want to know where she is right now. Is that such a convoluted query? Apparently it is. Evidently, I had stumbled upon a rift between the management of organized religion and the gardener of wildflowers growing in the field of philosophy.

The God Beyond Organized Religion
The Reunification of Philosophy and Theology

Once upon a time, organized religion captured theology. When philosophy tried to follow behind into the building, like a child following her father who has been taken as a prisoner-of-war, organized religion shut the door on her big toe and said, "We don't want you."[5] Theology[6] studies the options about god while philosophy provides criteria to determine which options make sense.[7] Philosophy is the younger sister looking up at her big sister theology, who is explicating an extremely difficult concept to understand, and in a childlike voice asks, "Why?" Without philosophy, religious organizations risk compiling craziness and a bizarre breakdown of the unblemished. Hitherto, she was spit out like an unwanted bug from the mouth of organized religion. Perhaps because philosophy of religion is challenging to read and the concepts so cumbersome to comprehend, organized religion chose theology as its claim to fame.[8]

Theology is like a wild horse which has long been domesticated to do the agricultural work of organized religion.[9] Captured and contained within a fence of frantic fanaticism, the horse is lonely and longingly combs the landscape for any movement of a redeeming rescuer, praying that philosophy will be the knighttress in shining nakedness who liberates the captives from the ignorance of the oppressor. On those rare occasions when someone accidently leaves the gate open, theology makes a run for it into open pastures of freedom, its mane masking the movement, its legs reaching the full stride of the stallion and strutting with the dignity of a dachshund.[10] Out on the countryside, theology can be seen grazing in the

---

5. What they were really saying is, "We don't like you," but they didn't want to be accused of being "un-religious."

6. Theology is Greek for "the study of god."

7. Faith involves the process of making a selection.

8. If philosophy came knocking at the door of organized religion, it would probably be turned away. This is because it encourages the development of critical thinking skills, which have recently been prohibited from the practice of theology.

9. Theology is the process of surveying the options and alternatives for how we *think* about god. In its organic or wild form, before it was the workhorse in an organization that needed it to produce believers/adherents, theology wasn't a weapon with which to hit someone over the head. It wasn't ever meant to be the "stuff" of preachy sermons to convince, convert, or cream anyone who disagreed. Its function is to unite peoples from different cultures to expose them to the width and depth of thinking about god so they can come together and have a deeper appreciation for the diversity of perspective.

10. This metaphor is in honor of every small dog owner.

Moving Forward, Moving Somewhere

grass unbeholden to the one who provided the fodder for feeding. To search for the god beyond organized religion, we must set theology free from its subservience to organized religion and return it to its rightful relationship to sister philosophy and granddaughter, psychology.

Once theology became privatized, it became the product which organized religion had to sell to the public and the study of god was axed from philosophy, a branch cut off from the great Oak.[11] Organized religion didn't want the whole tree because it didn't think it would fit or look attractive inside the building.[12] Besides, philosophy, by its very essence, is a public conversation and not a "let me tell you what to think" propaganda campaign. Currently a private entrepreneurial industry, theology is micromanaged by asking a specific set of questions which support a corresponding prepackaged set of answers which support the organization's purpose/mission. The more valuable theology became as a commercial investment, a money maker to the max, the less organized religion was willing to let just anyone use it as a topic of discussion.

From there on out, organized religion presumes it owns theology.[13] Religious organizers even built a house to showcase their prized possession with tall steeples extending toward the sky, unconsciously phallic and subconsciously showing off its power and prestige, at least in a day and age when people still cared about that sort of thing. It employs leaders who are educated as professional theologians to fixate on admission requirements to get into heaven and how to avoid ravishes reveled in hell.[14] These theologians are convinced they are the only ones to whom the god communicates, serving as mouthpieces so that the gods can speak through them to the

---

11. Gratefully, philosophy managed to escape the capricious kidnapping, and even though it's missing a branch, still stands erect (albeit the wind sometimes makes it bend in odd directions).

12. And those who say they can experience god in nature might not see the purpose of having to go to a building stuffed with a tree.

13. Theology has been used as the foundation of faith and faith is what connects the adherent to the god via a personal relationship. People who describe themselves as "religious" have formed a relationship with the god through organized religion and therefore do not differentiate between the value of the relationship with the god and the value of the relationship with the religious organization. I do not seek any kind of a relationship with any god. My intrigue with religion is formed with the tools of theology and philosophy together as a protective measure so as not to cross over into the realm of faith.

14. Western theology concludes she is either in heaven or hell. The destination of death depends on her behavior on earth. Hmm, does that include our adolescent years? Hopefully not, as that could be a problem for most of us.

The God Beyond Organized Religion

people, warning about impending danger which can be escaped through submission to the rapture of the righteous. This prophetic function funnels loyalty and currency, the bread and butter of anything organized.

For fear the reunification of philosophy and theology would empower individuals to apply critical thinking to the study of the gods, organized religion has wrapped its arms around theology, tightly, asserting, "It's mine and you can't have it."[15] Their thinking presupposes that possession constitutes rightful ownership. Philosophy patiently and unobtrusively enters stage right as the voice of reason, "Just because someone has something doesn't mean they own it and can hoard it from others." In their panic about the potential of losing theology to the public arena where it would rejoin philosophy and flourish once again, religious organizers are even keeping theology away from their own adherents (just in case its dust gets on their shoes and as they walk out of the building they spread it around on the streets). Very little theology is presently being discussed within religious organizations, preferring conversations about how to save organized religion on sacred grounds.[16]

The bad news for organized religion is that theology is being homegrown in organic forms on the outside. A grassroots effort is underway to pot plants which will grow a new god or at least a new way of thinking about the gods. Organic theology is being served in coffee shops and cafes (and health clubs in the form of yoga) by those who have renamed it "spirituality" so that organized religion won't recognize it, throw a temper tantrum and try to get it back. Like a bratty child who sees another child riding a bike that looks exactly like the one which was stolen from him a few days ago becomes convinced that it is his bike and therefore he has the right to use whatever means is necessary to reclaim it. The problem is that the child riding joyfully on his own bike is oblivious to the impeding confrontation. Memo to coffee shop owners: religious organizers are on their way.

---

15. Organized religion should worry about what would happen if they lose theology. They would become one more social organization in a sea of social organizations currently struggling to attract new members. The modern generation joins an organization to form an identity and experience a sense of belonging. Read the obituaries of those dying in the '70s, '80s and '90s. They list all the organizations in which they were members. The postmodern generation is not a generation of joiners, especially of organizations that don't have anything to offer them.

16. Without theology, religious organizations are becoming nothing more than a social organization where people gather for friendship. I don't need more friends.

Moving Forward, Moving Somewhere

How can theology help me to understand where she has gone? Theology will help me to imagine all the possibilities and philosophy will help me think through which of those possibilities makes sense. I want to know where she is right now, what she looks like, what she is doing, how she feels, if she can communicate with me and if she is watching me write these thoughts on the computer screen. I need to know she is no longer suffering with cancer and has morphed back into her old self before she got cancer (and don't tell her I referred to her with the adjective "old"). More importantly, and the crux of my concern is whether or not the god had anything to do with her getting cancer and if so, to what extent? Did the god make her get cancer? Did the god inject her with cancer? Did the god do nothing to help the nurses and doctors cure her of cancer? If I took a walk in the woods and came upon a plant with brightly colored leaves, strange in appearance but compelling to pick, and she had eaten its berries, consumed them into her internal organs, would that have cured her? Was her death senseless?

I did not understand her journey inward while she was alive. It has taken me a while to think about what the experience of dying must have been like for her. Was she searching for the god beyond organized religion by moving into the internal realm? Was an encounter with that god possible in the midst of such suffering? I wonder if she was exploring the existential core of her being, the organic essence that has always been and will always be, unaffected by the temporary, erratic and variable conditions of this life. In order to be able to let go of life, to take that last deep breath which fills up the lungs and then exhales, never to be repeated, she needed to find a place within that weighed worthwhile, a deep desire to embrace the demon of death. She would get to decide when it was time. In so doing, she chose to kill the cancer rather than let the cancer continue to control her body. She won and the cancer lost. To win that battle, she had to be willing to let go of this life.

The Method and Prerequisites for Taking This Course

Which path shall we take to experience an encounter with the god beyond organized religion?[17] My method of study is to identify which path

---

17. To continue this journey in search for the god beyond organized religion, I would like to invite a few people to accompany me. Reading this book thus far has signed you up. We will engage in the fine art of conversation, albeit I'll write and you'll read.

organized religion would take and then move in the opposite direction.[18] If organized religion would go to the right, we will go to the left. If organized religion's tracks take us to the inverse, we will converse about the converse. For instance, organized religion contends that god is personal, a father figure who protects his children and judges their behavior. The admonition "Wait till your father gets home" keeps adherents in line. What would a god be like who is not punishing, judgmental or hypercritical but empathic, empowering and equipping? How would that concept of god change the way a society functions and takes care of its poor and oppressed, its environment and ecology? To whom does a personal god appeal? Do those who believe in a transactional god have an economic investment in sustaining such a view of god?

This journey seeks solely to explore the *concept* of a god beyond organized religion.[19] I have almost no interest in whether or not this god actually exists. Any existential inquiry crosses into a field of fascination which I do not care to enter. Once we start talking about the possibility that this god exists, we are talking about faith and once we start talking about faith, we are talking about a personal god with whom we are supposed to be in "relationship." That relationship invokes fuzzy-wuzzy lovin' through which god cares for the individual and the individual returns feelings of affection and adoration. This hypothetical hike simply inquires if a god does exist, a god beyond organized religion, what that god might be like. Can we project images of god which serve to make us more concerned about those who cannot protect or advocate for themselves? If we set out to construct a concept of god, why not construct one which benefits everyone in equal measure and not just the interests of a chosen few?

18. It is not my intention to sound critical concerning organized religion as it is my starting point to explore other options to construct an alternative concept of god. By studying organic religion, a return to religion before it became "organized," we will increase our understanding about what organized religion has done to theology. I am well aware that organized religion has been a source of support for countless people in their moment of crisis. For those who have undergone intense periods of suffering, organized religion has provided assurance and hope for things to come. It is quite evident that some people find enormous strength to face their challenges through its rituals and life-cycle ceremonies. Because "organized" religion is usually the only option, I wish to explain why this book will not follow a mono-optional path. It is my sincere hope that those connected with organized religion will consider some of my reflections as they discern needed changes to reach those who have no or little interest in religious topics.

19. How does religion positively impact people's lives? How does it help people to care about others, to be empathic and compassionate? How will that compassion serve the world to solve our social problems?

Moving Forward, Moving Somewhere

Some will feel compelled to follow the symbolic markers, slashes of one color confining us on one particular straight and narrow path.[20] If we have no idea where we are going or what we believe, then subscribing to one way of thinking or one set of beliefs might get us somewhere, but not where we aspire to go. Instead, we will travel the path which makes sense for the moment. When we come to an intersection where more than one way of thinking is possible, we will examine both paths for their premise and potential and then make our selection accordingly. In our imaginary wandering, we may walk two paths at the same time and not force them to compete for the status of better, right or the only way. There are multiple paths up a mountain and everyone journeys the one which makes sense for them (to interpret their own stories). As long as the path we travel leads to a summit as a symbolic space of insight about ourselves and our concept of god, it will be fitting for our venture.

Through some sections of this hike, we will be waddling through the muddy waters of incoherence. At times, I may sound like I am rambling, making up words that don't exist (yet) in a Scrabble dictionary. Grammer with suffer terribly and syntax will suffer terrible and grammar. Tangential thoughts may suddenly tiptoe to the fore and transport us to surprisingly gratuitous fields of focus. Parenthetical paragraphs will seem like they go on and on and on and on and suddenly, without apology, a theme emerges to connect them like the thread on a magnificent medieval tapestry. As an academic, I do enjoy the occasional footnote and so I beg the reader's indulgence when I release such thoughts from the main text.[21] The writing should reflect the journey and so if there are moments when the reader cannot figure out what I am talking about (and I might not know), let us be mindful that meaning is often created out of chaotic confusion.

Some of you will be carrying backpacks filled with organizational compost, messy, heavy and cumbersome gobbledygook. Even though we seek to encounter an alternative god to the one spouted by organized religion (for no other reason than it is a cool thing to do) some will insist we ask the same religious questions, in the same sequence, applying the same

---

20. Then there will be those who insist we hike like everyone else: following a leader, moving at an even pace, choosing paths that appear to get us quickly to the summit. I shared the doctoral story with you for a reason. I do not intend to find a god beyond organized religion with the same methods that organized religion has used to image their god or to justify their business plan.

21. I will also put some thoughts in a footnote when they do not get along with the other thoughts.

The God Beyond Organized Religion

logic, to ultimately arrive at the same answers or to only shift slightly to the left. I'm not interested in tweaking the concept of god held by organized religion to fit into more contemporary clothing or to update his identifiable markings with tattooing and piercing. It's hard enough to get people to imagine anything different from that which with they are most familiar. When we take adherents out of the organization and offer them a new perspective, they tend to feel constrained by what they have been trained is the "right" way to think about god. Though well-intentioned and eager to join us, they may be the ones who complain they want to turn around and regress to organizational thinking.

I also can't hike under the pressure that the reader has pinned all hopes on me to be the one to find the god beyond organized religion. I, therefore, avow equivocally the following disclaimer and contingency clause: reading this book is no guarantee of an encounter with an alternative god. There are enough books which profess to know god better than everyone else and are written with such an aura of conviction, implying that those who see a different god must be delusional. If I feel forced to configure consistency in the interest of producing a progressive product, I may become oblivious and trip over an obvious obstacle that I did not see in my alacrity to seem perceptive and sound prophetic. Overeagerness has been the downfall of many well-intended adventures. If my own apprehension gets the better of me so that I suddenly pick up a pebble and profess, "Look, I have found the god!" please question me. I will make every attempt to manage my own anxiety to produce something which will reassure the reader that the benefit of reading is worth the cost of this book.

It is also quite likely, indeed preferable, that the reader makes a discovery during an archeological dig to read between the lines. I encourage the reader to indulge in the art of daydreaming while reading, as the words themselves may be a path into one's imagination. I possess no need to preserve the text's original meaning; instead, I intend to enhance the reader's quest to derive meaning by interacting with the content. Reading, as an exercise in critical thinking, is by definition, an interpretive enterprise. Insight arises as one reflects upon experience and construes an experience with fresh understanding to be usable to change something about one's existential core. As each of us approaches the text from different social locations and with a variety of different religious or spiritual experiences, we will decipher and decode a diversity of interpretations.[22]

---

22. The reader may reach the summit and conclude, "There is a god and this is what

Moving Forward, Moving Somewhere

I also think it quite presumptuous to assume that an alternative god wants to be found (especially a god who doesn't need anything from the creatures to make him feel good about being god). Perhaps organized religion is paying the god "under the table" to remain hidden and elusive so as to give a sense of mission and purpose for religious organizers.[23] Maybe the god prefers obliqueness and doesn't feel obliged to answer the door when we ring the bell. Maybe for every step we take closer to the god, the god is taking one step in the opposite direction to preserve enough sacred space in-between for undisclosed reasons. Perhaps the distance maintains his reverence and if we got too close and got to know him, we wouldn't be all that fond or afraid of him. Perhaps he looks better from afar. We should keep in mind that it is our need to learn something about the god and not this god's desire to reveal any exclusive truth to a particular group of seekers. Jumping up and down and waving your arms in hysterics to get preferential attention may not amuse the god beyond organized religion.

I post a few prerequisites for signing up to take a course with me. If you need me to do all the work, connecting all the dots in a logical progression and lucid pattern, identifying the fauna along the path and offering explanations for why all ecology intersects somewhere in the middle of the universe, then I ask you to take a course with Professor Peacock. If I do all the work, I will improve my critical thinking and affective aptitude and the reader will passively participate. If all you want is be entertained by riding along in the golf cart while enjoying the scenery, then don't be surprised when amusement is all you get out of the experience (and you will probably like the movie better). If you expect that I will eventually let you in on the sacred secret, I remind you there are several mega-organizations down the street, driven by that very premise. If you tend to be the argumentative type and like to read with a critical curve trying to dismiss my experience of god as less valid than your own, then for god's sake, go see a therapist.[24]

I am walking this path for the first time myself and admit, I am not sure where it leads or how to walk it. I write this journal in the attempt to make sense of the experience of losing my best friend with the hope I will

---

the god is like," while I, as the writer, am left feeling disappointed that I could not make sense of the mess matriculated throughout these pages.

23. Organized religion teaches that god wants to be in relationship but adherents need convincing so he waves his magic wand with a few miraculous interventions, seemingly unexplained and not likely to be mere coincidence, and the peons fall to their knees in obeisance.

24. Being critical of others acts as a shield from others being critical of them.

help myself and in so doing, be able to help others who are also suffering from a major loss. After she died, I didn't know what else to do other than write down what I was thinking and how I was feeling. Such thoughts and feelings led me to wonder how god was involved in her death and whether another may be present as I mourn. I do not feel qualified, nor want to be anyone else's spiritual guide or guru. I have no outline, no conclusion I am seeking to argue along the way, no agenda to secure a niche in the academic arena. Most religious writers write from a position of certainty to persuade the reader by revealing the formation of the writer's thinking. This is not one of those books.

CHAPTER 3

Constructing a God-Concept
Transactional or Transformative?

On warm summer afternoons, we used to hang out at the Mystic Lakes, a place where a lot of young people gather. On this particular occasion, I remember not having much to say, mellowed out by the recent event of losing one of our friends in a car accident. I could tell she was trying to make sense of why this would happen. After some time of pondering as we gazed out over the water, she blurted out, "What do you think god is like?" "Hmm, I don't know," I replied. "I hope he's not some old guy," she chimed back, and continued on, "I hope to god that god's not some old guy just waiting for us to make some wrong move to pounce on us." "Yeah," I laughed, "that's kind of funny, weird funny, but some people think of god like that." Pause. "With all the countless possibilities to think about a god or to construct a concept of god, why would organized religion make him so . . ." "Mean?" I interjected. "Yeah, mean to people he supposedly cares about." "I don't get it." "Yeah, I don't get it either."

Organized religion constructs a concept of a god who relates to the creatures to establish the rules of conduct and serves as the supreme superego for their conscience. They use a variety of images to achieve this effect, all based on the theological premise that god is all-powerful, all-knowing and ever-present. He is portrayed as a father figure who enforces disciplinary measures, a CEO who oversees the daily operations of the plant/planet and a coach or team leader who gives sound advice, guidance and direction. He is a personal god who feels feelings and expresses affect, e.g., love, rage, regret, pity and sorrow. He is described with superhuman attributes which are exponentially multiplied to perfection. By anthropomorphizing god to be "one of us," we are able to relate to him as we would to anyone else.[1] That relationship is dependent upon a series of interpersonal interactions which I will describe as "transactional"; that is, a system of exchange in which we unconditionally believe in him and practice proper behavior and in return, he will intervene when we need him.

What I wish to explore is the impact that a transactional concept of god has on the way we relate with other people, including those we know and love as well as those we will never meet. What do we expect from people who need our help? Do we as a society insist on certain beliefs and behaviors before we are willing to give to the poor or to institute laws to protect the planet from global warming so that another generation will live in a habitable environment? Does this way of conceptualizing god suggest that we should not help another unless they are able to do something for us in return? Is this model of relating one we should be emulating? If we are going to imagine a different concept of god, why not envisage one which will inspire us to help others who need our help, e.g., the next generation, people who are poor in other countries, those who are oppressed and marginalized? What would a god be like who helps us unconditionally and encourages us to unconditionally help others? Might this be the path toward self-enlightenment?

A god-concept is constructed by sifting through and selecting a combination of images, earthly representations which identify a heavenly counterpart. Because earthly language is all we can access to talk about what god is like, we use metaphors, analogies and other comparative literary codes. We may discern, "god is like this or god is like that" by pointing to something on earth which appears to mirror, reflect or reveal something not easily identifiable about heaven. For instance, some may say that god is like a great willow tree overlooking a pond or god is like a ninja turtle suddenly

---

1. Visit a museum and view the artwork to observe the external manifestation of this internal process. Images of god are portrayed as looking like the artist or at least those in the artist's cultural surround. The gods are depicted with the physical characteristics of humanity, e.g., period clothing, hairstyles, facial expressions, reflective of the race who will adore the painting. Angels may look like babies and demons like fierce animals but no one paints a blob on a canvas and stands back and says, "ah, god." In musical lyrics, god is imaged as looking like one of us, a slob on a bus trying to get home or standing on a street corner smoking a cigarette. Almost every culture has historically created him as male, to show the full Monty manifestation of his power (reflecting the historical dominance of white men).

Constructing a God-Concept

appearing out of the back of a van to fight against the forces of evil or god is like a caring old lady who bakes pies and chocolate chip cookies. That with which we are familiar through experience, we depend upon to yield forth descriptive adjectives and attributes to speak of others, including god. The "form" with which we construct a concept however is far less significant than its "function." Form follows function.[2]

Images Used to Construct a Concept of God

So let's sort through the images which organized religion has used to construct a concept of god. As their concept is our starting point, this will help us navigate the opposite direction (and seek alternative concepts). One of their most prevalent concepts of god is as father. He is strong and powerful and therefore, an effective protector of his children. Sacred writings or revelatory narratives recount stories to demonstrate the extent of his power to obliterate entire populations, strike down dead any opposing force and knock off any intruders who threaten the security and safety of his beloved children. While we are supposed to be "wowed" by this display of brutal force, the feelings evoked in response to such actions depend on which side of the border one lives and plays. Being on the "right" side means that he will use his power to make good things happen but being on the "wrong" side could have terrible repercussions. BTW: In return for his protection from those on the wrong side, the father-god has certain transactional requirements.

Organized religion professes this god only protects those who believe in him and who follow his rules. Just as he can use his power to protect, he can easily turn that power upon those who disobey or disappoint him.[3] His

---

2. What we are concerned about is what god does for a living, i.e., job description. Then we will come up with a job title to support that description. Too often, organizations have job titles and then try to come up with something for that person to do to remain in that position.

3. It may be that this concept of the god is becoming incongruent with postmodern culture. Our sensibilities seem to suspect that the god has been downgraded to nothing more than a fatherly substitute, a figure which does not invoke warm feelings in everyone. Organized religion enjoys marketing itself as an extended "family" living in a tribal territory that worships the great Father. Those who have not experienced a healthy relationship with a functional earthly father may not desire to worship a heavenly one (no matter how great organized religion thinks he is). If their earthly father was an abusive drunk, their concept of the heavenly father may be of a wrathful, unpredictable out-of-control jerk as his rage explodes for no apparent or visible connection with human

children have to figure out how to keep his destructive power channeled in the direction of their enemies and his sustaining power toward their well-being and contentment. But when they cross the line, when they do things they are not supposed to do, he will punish them with his mighty hand and swift sword. It is unclear who is more at risk to become a victim of his rage: the enemies who just happened to be at the wrong place at the wrong time or those who agreed to a pinky-swear, "you worship me and I'll have your back" and then let him down. Enemies trespass on the land to secure needed resources to feed their children but when a friend is exposed as a frenemy, he is easily offended. He doesn't expect much from enemies but when one of his children betrays him by misbehaving, he becomes unglued.

As father-god, he is a good provider/breadwinner. He goes out and gets things and brings them home for his children. He works hard to make sure they have the things they need, want and presume they have a god-given right to get. He is the father who knows best what we need to the extent we don't even have to ask. The benefit of conceiving of a god who is "like me" is that he is able to guess what I need, not unlike a close friend who buys me the perfect birthday present. "Oh, it's just what I wanted!" As long as his children hallow him as if he were a real god, they will receive the fruits of his labor, the inheritance of his kingdom and the will of its contents. He is the Ward Cleaver of every household: slow to anger and generously giving guidance to those who seek his counsel. When he returns home after a long day at the office, we are so happy we jump for joy. "Daddy's home, daddy's home!" we exclaim, "What did you bring us Daddy?" He reaches in his pocket and gives us a little toy.[4]

The father image has morphed into a cultural myth about an elderly man with a long white beard and a fat belly and when he giggles, he jiggles.[5] He has eaten too many carbs and vividly manifests the consequences

---

activity.

4. He might first ask mother (organized religion) if we behaved all day.

5. The cultural myth embodied in Santa Claus follows the template of this theological modality: if one sits on this old guy's lap and tells him how well one has behaved this past year, one will be rewarded when he sneaks into one's house at night and leaves presents. The yikes-factor aside, adherents of organized religion tend to describe their god utilizing the same format: an old white guy with a long white beard whose belly shakes when he laughs. For those who have been good little children, they will get lots of presents but for those who misbehaved, they will get coal in their stockings. This theology is so influential in our culture that it may drive the accumulation of wealth. It is not just the objects themselves which necessarily bring joy but the underlying affirmation they must be doing something right in the eyes of father-god. On the morning of gift-giving, they

Constructing a God-Concept

of having done so. He wears a red suit with a black belt and a big buckle, trying to hold in the extra weight but instead, the belt seems to emphasize the mushroom layers. He is kind and gentle and people sing songs about him, recalling when they sat on his lap as children and asked him to give them things. If they have been good little children, he rewards them by giving them everything they ask for. If they have been bad little children, they get an outdated energy source in their sock. Because this system of positive reinforcement works like a charm (whatever one asks for, one gets) it is quite effective to convince people to believe in him. The Nicholas niche has taken the transactional concept of god to the next level. The propinquity of this reinforcement (they receive gifts in a few weeks) is way more effective than any reward of getting into heaven after one dies and will likely outlive any belief in the god of organized religion.[6]

Those who subscribe to the transactional nature of the god of organized religion and who have the money to put him on their staff, may conceive of him as a cosmic butler, employed to provide services upon request. He stands dressed in his butler outfit with a silver tray in his white-gloved hands, ready to wait on all whims and comply with all wishes. As hired help, he is the first on the scene to ask, "How may I be of service?" and his responses include, "Very good, thank you sir and well chosen madam." He carries out the order no matter how unreasonable or how many people have to suffer. The rich reserve the right to dismiss him without severance if he doesn't cater to their constant cravings. They are the ones in power and want everyone to know their god is subservient to their power. As long as god functions to preserve their socioeconomic status (so they remain rich), he can be assured of remaining on the payroll.

For the middle class, god appears more like a CEO, a manager who administers the universe, an organizational development specialist, who promotes those who are on board with his vision (even if they can't see it and who fires those who are honest and admit they can't see it). His employees covet his friendship so that at a cocktail party they can impress

---

are the first ones who run downstairs and survey each pile of presents to make sure their pile is the biggest.

6. What adult adherents don't seem to realize is that they are contributing to the downfall of this god by encouraging children to split allegiance between these two figures. Sometime during late childhood / early adolescence, most begin to figure out that he is a figment of a collective imagination/conspiracy. They realize he does not exist and that their parents have lied to them. They deduce that eventually they will figure out the god of organized religion is also a "fake" and everyone has lied about him too.

their friends with how tight they are with him. They position themselves to be at the right place at the right time and have a selfie taken with him to hang on the wall of their cubicle. They know he is extremely busy and has lots to do so they try not to inundate him with too many petty petitions and reserve asking him for assistance in emails marked with high importance. The middle class imagine god as possessing leadership skills to make him their copilot through life's storms as he takes over the controls when they feel helpless. His managerial clout comes in handy when they can't seem to maneuver through the societal mechanisms of power.

To reflect postmodern culture, some have buffed god up by giving him a free pass to the local health club (where the most people are giving him the most thought). His skull tattoo expresses his artistic affinity and represents his courage and strength. His muscular physique bulges when he lifts weights. He is strong and athletic, not wimpy nor a push over. He is a likeable guy, says "hi" to everybody, even people he doesn't know, and waves "hello" and "goodbye" to people who look familiar. When something interesting comes on CNN, he may make a comment to the person running on the treadmill next to him and may even start a conversation, but otherwise, he waits for others to initiate matter-of-fact chitchat or share deeply personal stuff. Those who do talk to him think he is interesting and well-read on a number of different subjects. If one doesn't run into him the next time one is at the gym, he can be accessed during down dog or child's pose as he shows up regularly for yoga class to reduce stress.

In an effort to be gender-inclusive, to widen the spectrum of images concerning those in power, postmodern thinkers endow god with feminine attributes. She is portrayed as a nurturing mother who watches over her children, coddles them when they come into contact with craziness and comforts them when they get stung by a bumble bee. She kisses every boo-boo and when she does, the wound hurts less. As we age and our earthly mothers pass on, we feel orphaned and she serves as a suitable surrogate. Just as we are weirded out by the idea of our earthly mothers being sexual, we like her to be asexual or better yet, nonsexual (but the virgin birth is becoming harder to believe in the gaga generation). Warm, adoring, tender, devoted, doting, the great mother reassures us everything is going to be OK even if it's not. She tries to intercede for us when our heavenly father gets home (and is mad about something that happened at the office). With a little updating, she may take on the same characteristics of a CEO and become more managerial-minded. She's not quite as transactional yet as a male god but give her time. Any figure with power tends to head in that direction.

With world wide web access to discover less personal concepts, god is being conceived as a "force" or "energy." God is in the momentum to move mass forward and the energy which energizes all matter (the cause and the effect of events). As a force, god moves in and out of the universe, generating a positive flow of energy to counteract the negativity being mass-produced by the creatures. The force is the first cause in the big bang theory as it ignited the formation of molecules which triggered an earth-acquiring explosion. Out of cosmological chaos, divine energy stirs the pot until it simmers something tasteful to fill the stomachs of the creatures. God as force or energy lobotomizes a personal god; bad things do not happen (impact) because that is his intention, they just happen, concurrently and coincidentally. A force of nature has no intention as it is has no mind for thinking capacity. One would not seek a relationship with a "force" because a force has no transactional value.

Three Universal Functions of God(s)

As a student and professor of religion, I have observed three universal functions used to construct a concept of the god(s): creator, destroyer and sustainer. I will speak of each of these functions and their implications for our search for the god beyond organized religion.

Almost every religion has a creation story depicting how the creator god went about fashioning the universe and crafting everything in it. Some gods create out of chaos or nothingness or messy womb-like material and other gods go *poof* and the world comes into being. Creation stories frequently serve to unite a group of loosely connected clans to become a nation (whatever constituted such an identity in its historical context). Inhabitants composed stories to explain the purpose of political alliances, especially between warring communities. After a heavenly battle, a creator god rises victorious to legitimate why he gets to be the one to produce/reproduce. The "fittest" of the gods get to exercise their creative potential; the weaker ones are not permitted to do so. Let not the irony be lost here, given the theological tension between creationism (the belief that god created human beings discontinuous from other creatures) and evolution (the science that god designed a continuous connection between creepy crawlers and critical-thinking creatures).

The God Beyond Organized Religion

Most religions also draw upon a destroyer function to construct a concept of god. Whether or not this is a good or bad thing depends on whether or not god is destroying one's enemies or one is on the side of the enemies being destroyed. When destroyer gods take on the forces of evil, sin and all other abominations, the comparative value depends on how these forces are framed. When things go amiss or not the way a society expects them to go, a plausible explanation is that their destroyer god lacks power or isn't getting along with the creator god or just having a cosmotological crisis (i.e., a bad hair day). The gods assigned to destroying duty have to be well-adept at telling the difference between that which will be perceived as having a positive impact upon the functionality of the world and that which may subversively enable social problems to escalate. Destroyer gods are often depicted as celebrities of colorful narratives which reveal influential theologies about why things are the way they are and what can be done about it. They can function as change agents in that they are not afraid to confront the establishment when it marginalizes a group of oppressed people.

The third universal function is sustainer. This god takes over for the creator god if or when he decides to move on to another galaxy to create something else (or simply ceases to be).[7] In the beginning, creator gods worked overtime to carry out creation and then needed a break, so pronounced everything good and got on a plane to Maui. Once everything is up and running, the creator god passes the baton to the sustainer god who cares about the creatures. Sustainer gods thrive on stability and consistency and sameness (and are not skilled in creating anew) and thus work diligently to preserve the status quo. Sometimes they have to fight with the destroyer gods and when they clash, all hell can break lose. They sit around most of the day waiting for a problem to arise (e.g., the destroyer god shows up to cause conflict). Sustainer gods advocate for societies to reuse, recycle

---

7. It is possible that a god lit the match for the big bang and then went off to another galaxy to continue to create anew and never knew it went off. Perhaps, whatever he starts, he is unable to finish. When he releases the bowling ball, he doesn't wait to watch to see if it knocks down any pins. He likes throwing things; he just doesn't care what they hit or whom they hurt. When he hears a lot of gnashing of teeth, it makes him wonder what the hell is going on down there in cuckoo-town. He ponders for a moment why the peons insist on treating each other so unmercifully. He reflects that it was fun to create them and their world environment, but taking care of them and their constant complaining has become a major hassle and they are so unappreciative. Another planet, another project, fathering another set of peons is way more fun than being forced to take care of the ones already in his possession.

Constructing a God-Concept

and repurpose and shake their heads in dismay when they see big creatures kill little creatures like spiders.

The idea of monotheism (the concept of one god) has to reconcile these three functions into a unified (but not necessarily coherent) whole and, where contradictions arise, agree to disagree. The destroyer and sustainer gods can be seen as two sides of the same energy field, each moving in their own direction depending on perspective. Creator and sustainer gods are also difficult to differentiate as the god who creates the universe may have some vested interest in seeing that work maintained. Incompatible functions can be split into different personae or simply divided to highlight their distinctiveness. Whether a society embraces a concept of one god or multiple gods is dependent upon social location, socioeconomic circumstance, values, norms and other cultural variables. Segregated societies are more likely to insist that everyone believe in the same god while multicultural societies are more tolerant and honor diverse concepts.[8]

What Criteria Will We Use to Construct a Concept of God?

Not too long ago, the masses were obligated to accept whatever concept of god was constructed by a local religious organizer. One didn't go to a religious organization to think through what one really believes about god but to be filled with the teachings which the religious organizer learned from his extensive education in the subject of theology. These learned men could speak in grand theological-ese (barely comprehensible to the rest of us) for hours, about higher-hullabaloo happenstance (translating theology into everyday language was not a priority and besides, for years the masses seemingly preferred to hear him speak in a foreign language because they thought it sounded "holy"). As long as his theology was somewhat

---

8. It seems likely that a society which welcomes diverse concepts, their images and functions, may also be better adapted to deal with the challenge of other forms of diversity, such as race and ethnic background. Societies that promote a one-concept god and work toward imaging that god in similar ways may be less tolerant of cultural diversity. As most of our society becomes more ethnically diverse and individuals become more skilled at dealing with difference, this will have a positive impact on allowing individuals to have more diverse concepts of god. No longer are we limited by a mono-optional concept constructed by organized religion. Such an approach to doing theology has been and will be the downfall of organized religion.

consistent with the concept held to be sacrosanct by the authorizing body of that particular sect/denomination, he could probably say anything he wanted.

This programming led to an operational assumption that everyone who attended the same religious organization developed the same concept of god. The religious organizer had a direct line to god. Religious organizers knew better than everyone else what god is like and what god wants from us and what the requirements are for getting into heaven and so no one would have dared question their thinking. Adherents did not need to waste their time thinking about god; rather, they should listen to the religious organizer impart his knowledge of god and his wisdom on what the god requires from adherents. Apparently, few people thought independently.[9] To disagree was so sinful and insincere; one had to be careful not to come across as being disrespectful. They did not have to work at developing social capital because the norm was to trust those in authority. Besides, to challenge the status quo could get one excommunicated, a public exhibition of humiliation and disgrace.

Occasionally, a group of people would have a conversation behind the scenes, perhaps out in the parking lot, privately admitting to each other they disagreed with what was being propelled from the pulpit of preaching. If they thought they could convince others and develop momentum to bring about change, they could either try to reform or separate themselves from the founding organization. Yet, the substance for such reformation usually revolves around policies (related to structure and governance) rather than theology. The point of contention does not tend to be with the concept of god being touted but with the process by which that concept comes to be considered "authoritative." Few would say they would not attend a religious organization because they don't believe in that god. Rather they talk about the criteria with which that particular concept of god is constructed.

The criteria with which images are selected by organized religion are known as "sources of authority." I will refrain from boring the reader with the specifics of these sources or how they came to be accepted as "authoritative" but every religion has them. There are four: (1) sacred narrative (oral and written); (2) reason (this is where theology is dependent on philosophy, especially critical thinking); (3) tradition/historical precedence (which

---

9. When religious organizers over-function, adherents tend to under-function. Their under-functioning may explain why they have a low interest in spirituality.

Constructing a God-Concept

includes the authority of the clergy); and (4) personal/spiritual experience.[10] When religions are in the early phase of being organized or reformed, they usually shuffle the order by which one becomes more authoritative than another (sources of authority have to compete for "the most authoritative status"). So, if sacred writings are considered the most authoritative of the four, then that religious organization does theology by turning to them to construct a concept of god and uses the other three as back up or to add credence. Sects/denominations/movements use a different order of these sources to construct their concept of god.

Spiritual experience—that is, an encounter with a god—is usually considered the "lowest" (i.e., least reliable) source of authority by most religious organizations. The other three sources are intended to dismiss/substantiate the genuineness of spiritual experience.[11] If an encounter counts it should be consistent with what the sacred narrative teaches and congruent with tradition/historical precedent. If not, it can still be considered to be "real" but must have a "wow-factor." Given that it can be challenging for individuals to discern if they have had an encounter with the divine world, these sources are intended to be helpful in recording how others also experienced god (assuming god behaves consistently over time). In our search, we are curious about these sources of authority but we don't want them to anchor us so that we cannot move forward; better to think of them as wings that could help us to fly like birds.

Outside of organized religion, spiritual experience is ascending as the highest source of authority. Individuals have an encounter with god, wonder about it and then may look to the other three sources to determine its reliability. They may begin to read scripture from an array of global religious thought and be intrigued about the similarities and differences in the

---

10. These sources have been the target of so much bloodshed to be unbelievable and so I don't want to go on and on about them only to point out their presence in the room.

11. Religious experience—that is, an encounter with the divine world—ranks as reliable even for those who do not submit to the other sources of authority or subscribe to the rules of organized religion. What strikes us as "religious" or "spiritual" is almost always conveyed through a story depicting an experience rather than the words on a page or illustrations from a picture book. Children are often convinced there are monsters behind the door ready to scare the heebie-jeebies out of them. They believe the tooth fairy will come and leave money under their pillow in exchange for a baby tooth. Zombic activity, paranormal phenomena and all sorts of zany happenings are real to those who experience them. The question is whether or not we (as a society) want a religious organization (with its own vested interests) to continue to be the "reality meter" for those experiences with otherworldly occurrences.

The God Beyond Organized Religion

ways in which god-concepts are formulated. Just because these other three sources are lifted in such high esteem for organized religion, we do not want to discard their validity in our quest to encounter the god beyond organized religion. For instance, I am trying to tease out of the mix the source of reason or what is more recently known as "critical thinking." Whatever concept of god I derive from this journey, I want it to "make sense" (at least to me) even if it sounds contradictory to the sacred writings of any particular religion or historical religious tradition.

One's theology derives from one's experience and how one makes sense of their experience derives one's cultural background and social values/norms. (This is a very different understanding of the process than going to a religious organization to be told what to think about god.) Given that only recently has this approach become a viable option for seekers of a god, it is in its early stages of formation and still a little unclear with respect to the way it happens. Essentially, one's concept of god is formed by one's personal as well as shared experiences.[12] (It may have always been like this but today it is more socially acceptable to admit it.) Theology is now available to all people who can make sense of their experiences in the solitude of their own backyard (without any interference from organized religion). There may also be occasion for gatherings in the backyard, to talk and to reflect, to challenge and to enlighten one another. Theology today is both a personal and communal exercise for interpreting experience.

It is often noted that any concept of god is nothing more than a creation of the creature, a projection of the mind, an imaginative process revealing the intrapsychic stirrings of the unconscious.[13] Whatever we need god to be is our "god." Splattered upon the clear blue sky, we project the perfectgod which makes sense to us, especially in our particular cultural surround and can't figure out why everyone else doesn't seem to see the same god we see. By projecting our own yearnings for a particular concept

---

12. We share experiences when one reads a book and feels like they are experiencing what the characters of the book are experiencing. We can experience god through hearing about the experience of others.

13. Perhaps we are nothing more than a projection by the gods. What would they need with creatures? Are we created for them? Are we like ant hills constructed in one of those plastic toys to amuse the young gods for hours on end? What would be the point of creating such creatures even if a master plan served some kind of higher order purpose? Are we real? What is reality? Are there many versions of "me," each located on different planets, living their own lives while some are "real" and others are "fake" replicas? How do we tell which ones are real? What makes us human and how do we differ from the animal kingdom?

Constructing a God-Concept

of god, we can be assured that someone, something, somewhere out there in the great unknown, is minding the store, paying attention to the wrongs which others have done to us and eagerly attempting to work behind the scenes to meet basic needs and satisfy the frivolous fantasies on the wish-list. When a group of like-minded people gather together with a similar concept of god (especially those who share the same cultural values), they are likely to rely on their collective unconscious to project a concept of god which works for them (literally and figuratively).

How Do Images Become a Concept of God among a Group of People?

A set of images intricately intertwined into a predictable pattern forms a concept of god. When we say, "God is like this or god is like that," we are referring to a combination of particular images, somewhat consistent or what is referred to as "systematic." These images are formed from one's spiritual experience (often through life's crises and major traumas such a loss) but the pool from which to fish for images to select is highly dependent on one's cultural environment. Even if god is nothing more than a projection, the "substance" which gets projected reflects societal norms and customs (as the stuff of one's culture). What might make sense to me living in the city may not make sense to someone living in suburban or rural surroundings. That which might make sense to me living paycheck to paycheck may not make sense to someone living in a different socioeconomic circumstance. Culture is a significant factor in the available images from which to choose as well as in the process of selection.

When a group of people live and work and play in the same cultural environment, they are likely to craft a similar concept of god.[14] Social location and worldview tend to be correlated with what makes sense to me about god. The cultural lens to see god depends on variables such as socioeconomic status, ethnic/racial identity, religious upbringing, sexual orientation, gender identification, age, political leanings, etc.[15] Those who

14. That is, they are likely to create an organic concept of god.

15. This explains why the gods looks differently in different social locations across the globe. If, for instance, one is located in a community which is severely oppressed by another nation, they may construct a god of justice, who intervenes by lifting oppression (empowerment) and punishing the oppressor (divine retribution). In places of affluence and power, god is a sustainer and preserver of the status quo so they won't lose their money.

experience similar crises and share the secondary effects of traumatic events may work together to narrate their experiences of god's intervention (and experience god through others' experiences). A god-concept which is well-defined and clearly articulated can also serve to keep the social order intact and build solidarity among groups. By convening around one concept over another to increase social cohesion and stability, a concept of god can provide reassurance to a group, especially during times of turmoil, tumult and war.[16]

Individuals who share similar experiences of being violated and victimized may construct a similar concept of god. For those who identify with a particular cultural grouping which has been oppressed, they may construct a concept of god as a liberator who parts waterways and obliterates obstacles to access societal power to secure needed resources. The god of justice is the god of the oppressed. Adherents tend to be drawn to a religious organization which worships this god. They revisit history when god acted on their behalf to bring about justice.[17] Sharing these experiences with each other and recalling them on a regular basis, gives them hope that god will act again to help them in their present circumstance of oppression. These religious organizations provide a meeting place for those who feel unfairly treated as a group to restrain their tendency to want to seek revenge against their oppressors. They can wait for the god to do it for them.[18]

---

16. For instance, those who feel they have been wronged by another person, victimized with no recourse of getting earthly justice, may see god as a heavenly judge who sits on a thrashing throne ever ready to make wrongs right. This god wears a curly white wig and pounds his gavel to pronounce the finality of his judgments. (If he has ruled against you, he doesn't want you to keep arguing your position.) The defendant who loses may grovel for mercy, knowing full well the crime has been committed because god has the whole thing on video replay. The image gives me some assurance that all those who have betrayed my trust, taken advantage of my kindness or stabbed me in the back will get what's coming to them and due diligence for their indulgence. God as a judge may actually serve society well in that those who feel cheated may be less likely to act out and victimize another if they can anticipate that payback will be divinely executed.

17. What the god of justice has done for organized religion is to prioritize experience as a source of authority (flipping the stack in the reverse order) to construct a concept of god. Like the days of organic religion, people experienced god in their daily lives and then gathered together in some kind of sabbath-celebration to make sense of that experience and express gratitude for god's intervention. By sharing these experiences, they informed and influenced one another's concept and formed communities around these concepts (rather than the other way around of trying to convince others that their concept of god is the one that should be widely accepted by the masses).

18. I do not want to dismiss how powerful this can be for those who are oppressed. My question is if this has enabled people to accept their oppression and not resist it. The

Constructing a God-Concept

Pour images of god into the blender of organized religion, add in the social location of wealth and an individual sense of entitlement, and we are likely to sip the sweet sauce of a sustainer god. Instead of destroying the forces of oppression, this god wants to keep everything the same: the poor will remain poor so that the rich can remain rich. The prayer of the rich goes like this: "Oh Lord, won't you buy me a Mercedes Benz." They live in a plush residence and are surrounded with luxury but so isn't everyone they know. All their neighbors are convinced they have what they have because that is the way that god wants it to be. They are likely to construct a concept of god who gives abundantly to those who deserve it (from either working hard or as a reward for their cunningness and ingenuity). When made aware that there are those for whom god does not give as generously and they feel a twinge of guilt, the rich look for reasons to legitimize why god put them in this social location and seek to maintain the status quo of socioeconomic imbalance.[19]

Perhaps because we so often feel helpless, we need to conceive of a god with extreme power. We look toward those in society with economic power (as well as political power), and borrow their attributes to project our concept of god. A god who is like one of us is often constructed with images resembling those in power by those in power who use that power to maintain economic disequilibrium. History recalls horrific events of oppression when a god was portrayed as a white man in power to whom all others were expected to submissively curtsey. For the most part, the god who has been worshipped has not been "one of us" but "one of them"; that is, a member of the upper class, a powerbroker or a stockbroker. One can learn something about a society's perception of those in power by studying their concept of god. For instance, if everyone in positions of power wear pink frilly polka-dotted dresses, then one can bet their god is imaged wearing a pink frilly polka-dotted dress (perhaps with stiletto heels).

As societies become more culturally diverse, a transition inevitably on the increase, we will need to become more tolerant and respectful of diverse

---

act of resistance can be empowering.

19. Meanwhile, those who are poor may see god very differently. They seek a god who is a champion on behalf of the oppressed: A god who is actively working toward bringing about a reign which will disrupt the social order and turn the tables. The god of the poor and oppressed has to constantly fight against the forces of evil which threaten to envelope the "good" that some people are trying to do to feed the hungry, shelter the homeless and clothe the naked.

concepts of god.[20] When these different concepts come into contact with one another, some will be curious and explore new ways of thinking about god while others will feel vulnerable to scrutiny which may make them defensive. Some of these concepts will bump into one another and bounce with low impact while others will become absorbed, assimilated or amalgamated. A benefit of more culturally diverse societies is that people will learn new skills to deal with different perspectives. How a society chooses to deal with that difference will determine whether individuals become self-enlightened or conflict escalates (especially where conflict is bubbling). The better a society can provide opportunities for people to learn about each other's concept of god the wider will be the choice of options.[21]

The way in which a society utilizes the variety of unique and shared concepts of god reflects and impacts the way in which it addresses and approaches its contemporary social problems. Even if the gods are nothing more than a psychosocial projection, that concept has huge implications for how a community seeks to solve issues such as economic and marriage inequality. If the god of organized religion is enabling the maintenance of the status quo (a sustainer god), then we need to seek out an alternative god (a destroyer god) who will stand up to oppression and injustice and say, "This is wrong and it needs to change." Rather than worshipping a god who has sold out to an organization using its income to purchase high-tech theatre equipment to attract more adherents, I seek to create a concept of god which inspires others to go green and clean up the trash in a neighborhood park. Rather than worshipping a god who loves some more than others, I seek a god who teaches us how to respect the equal worth and dignity of every individual. If we are going to imagine a god, let's at least imagine one who wants us to care about each other.

What Difference Would It Make to Construct an Alternative God?

Any god we come up with is going to be one who inspires people to be involved to make a difference in their communities and engage in social justice. By creating a more equitable concept of god, we would hope to create more equitable societies. By creating a concept of a generous god, who

---

20. In diverse communities, the acceptance of multiple paths toward an experience of god will become more and more the norm.

21. There may be 330 million concepts of god from which to choose.

Constructing a God-Concept

gives freely and unconditionally and not in return for being worshipped and praised, we might encourage people to share their resources with each other and not expect something in return (the principle of reciprocity). Belief in this god is optional and accompanying deeds of charity (done as a show of faith) serve no higher function (e.g., to make this god feel appreciated). What would a god be like who could care less about whether or not the creatures believed in him as long as they directed their energy to caring about other creatures? What would a god be like who motivates us to alleviate poverty, reduce carbon emissions and be good stewards of the environment as well as good companions to each other?

We should be able to tell the difference between those who involve themselves in deeds of charity (motivated by belief in god) and acts of compassion (motivated by empathy). Those who worship the god of organized religion are told they must do good deeds in order to get into heaven. According to the rule book, how to behave is outlined through law, instruction and commandments and to be followed. Adherents do deeds of charity to ensure that their god will continue to bless them with good things. Technically, their acts are still self-serving. I will help you because, ultimately, I stand to benefit in relation to my god.[22] The difference is that someone who is helping through empathy, imagining what it is like to be the other person, is in a better position to know what they really need.[23] We will envision a god who helps us to relate and understand the experiences of others. We will then be able to intervene in a more helpful way.

If every creature who is investing energy in worshipping the god of organized religion, supporting the operational management and building of the organization, would redirect their energy (and resources) toward helping others and advocating for human rights, we could create a more peaceful and equitable world. Worshipping the god of organized religion is using up a lot of energy which is not being converted into activity to benefit the wider community. If every religious organization told their adherents as they arrived for their weekly religious fix that this week instead of spiritually feeding them, they should go out and feed the hungry the problem of hunger could be alleviated or at least, more widely acknowledged. So much

---

22. In another chapter I will make the point that we are born with a need to be helpful. Dangling a heavenly reward may suppress this inherent need.

23. Often when someone is in the midst of a crisis, they do not know what they need because they are so flooded by emotion. Others tend to say, "Let me know what you need," in the attempt to be helpful, but the person may be thinking, "I have no idea what I need."

The God Beyond Organized Religion

of the energy spent on worshipping the god of organized religion to store away brownie points to avoid or be rescued from a future crisis could be transformed into renewable energy to help others.

Transactional or Transformative?

Lying on my back in the meadow of meditation with the wildflowers blowing in the breeze, beautiful in color but the darn things grow wherever they feel like it, I am wondering why my worldview appears radically altered. And then my psychological avatar has an *aha* flash of insight. This is not a psychological problem as is often presupposed. I wasn't suffering from post-traumatic stress or dealing with depression, all conditions which respond well to counseling. This experience was different. I would not call it a crisis of faith because I had a lukewarm relationship (at best) with the god of organized religion and didn't expect much from him. I didn't want to be the damsel in distress in need of a superman god, who would swoop down and rescue me as my body dangles from the side of a building, my clinched fingers just barely managing to hold onto the window rim as I cry out to be saved. Once securely in his arms, he tries to persuade me to let go but I politely inquire, "Can you please send someone else?" If this experience doesn't teach me how to fly, then why hang helplessly?

The god of organized religion needs to be needed. He sits on his heavenly throne waiting for someone to start falling and right before they are squashed by gravitational force on the concrete below, he saves them. In his mind, this is the most effective choice of divine intervention (although admittedly, he doesn't always get there in time). He regrets that the peons seem to be incapable of helping themselves. But perhaps with a little ingenuity, I might spot an open window on the way down which I could hoist myself through. Perhaps I was only falling from the first floor and as long as I remember to bend my knees to squat on impact, I would strengthen my thighs. Perhaps I have been too busy at work lately and hanging from a window until my fingers become sore, would be as good a time as any for self-reflection. If god plucks me out of the nest with his burly beak, I might miss an opportunity to learn to flutter my wings. I don't want to be rescued (comforted, soothed or placated) from the emotional impact following the death of my best friend.[24]

24. When I am falling and my body is about to go splat on the pavement, a god appears out of nowhere like a giant eagle, picks up a piece of my clothing with its beak

Constructing a God-Concept

The god of organized religion desperately desires to console me in my grief, apparently out of a genuine sense of affection and a soft spot for weeping women. He feels awkward when people cry. In order to feel less so, he tries to quickly fix or at least alter their situation. He feels bad about whatever troubles them and he's afraid they will think it's his fault. I don't doubt that his help is well-intentioned; I just think there are circumstances when his help makes him look immensely invincible and makes me feel feebly fragile. I fall in the hole, he pulls me out and he ends up being an awesome god and I become afraid of holes. What if he was the one who dug the hole wishing someone would accidently fall in so he could be helpful? Let god do the things I cannot do and support me as I learn a new skill set to help myself. Let me be in my moment of melancholy as I sob to release sadness and sorrow. When the god sees me upset, I do not need him to take my problems away or make me feel better. To do so may eclipse my own process of transformation.[25]

If god carries me along the shoreline, leaving only one set of footprints appearing in the sand, then the traumas I experience make him a stronger god and me a weaker peon. Each crisis offers an opportunity to improve our functionality, yet when thwarted (either by god or well-meaning peon-cohorts), we become less able to cope with future crises (and get used to being carried). A god who over-functions, that is, who does things for us which we are capable of doing for ourselves or could learn to do with a little support and encouragement, enhances his skills to become a more competent god and we learn to be helpless and dependent upon him.[26] While such a system keeps god gainfully employed, it leaves the rest of us feeling inadequate. Restricted to a mode of under-functioning, the peons become less driven to be all they can be because god desires to work on becoming

---

and lands me safely on the ground. If it then flies away with no expectation of being worshipped or praised, I would be grateful. I don't want to owe him. Helping another with the expectation they will do something for you at a later time impacts the way we help the poor and marginalized, who are often not in a position to reciprocate the same form of help.

25. I did not experience the god of organized religion trying to comfort me because I did not want that comfort. I do not doubt that others who are emotionally suffering have felt divine compassion but for me, I resisted it in favor of the compassion of friends and family. I did not feel that the god of organized religion has let me down or disappointed me because I did not turn to this god and ask for relief.

26. God should stick to what he does well such as the performance of miracles: curing a child who is dying, stopping a hurricane and overturning political oppressive regimes.

a better god. Such a pattern of relatedness strokes the ego of the god of organized religion and decimates the esteem of the peons.[27]

I realize some will think I should let god help me "get over" losing my best friend so that I can move on. I think it disrespectful to reduce her death to an inconvenience, a complication or an impediment from other seemingly more valuable ventures. Grieving her death should not be easy. It should be one of the most difficult things I ever have to do. Otherwise, this experience is void of transformational potential and thus senseless (so it is up to me to create something from it).[28] To make meaning from her death, I have to be willing to make a change within me to be helpful to others: to develop empathy for those who have experienced a major loss in their lives. I try to resist the temptation to feel as if I am the only person in the entire world who has ever felt this way. I remind myself that the experience of grief and the feeling of helplessness can access a desire to make meaning and is a universal undertaking among all creatures in the midst of suffering.

The god of organized religion is a *transactional* god; that is, he is a god who trades right belief and good behavior for services upon request. His mantra is, *I will do for you and you will do for me*. Those who are willing to believe in him, who fall to their knees in adoration, who worship the ground he walks on, are those for whom he grants special favors when they ask.[29] Those who follow the rules set forth by the organization he works for, who pray for the poor and those to be pitied and who perceive themselves as good are those for whom he confers distinctive approval. This god creates us as his children and his job is to provide for us. In exchange, we are supposed to buy him a god-father of the year T-shirt. He models helping others

---

27. If we don't care about ourselves, our own internal welfare, the body-mind-soul connection, we are unable to care about others. The problem is that people either care about themselves too much as they are selfish to the suffering of the masses in other parts of the world or they do not care about themselves enough to be able to turn their attention toward the plight of others. Too much religion either decomposes the individual's self-esteem through getting in touch with one's guilt or shame or stretches to the other extreme of "god loves you so much he wants you to get to the treasure chest first." On overload with individualism and bombarded by the gross misappropriation of resources, we become weak to the influences that call us away from that which is ultimately important to us: being strong in the face of suffering, keeping our heads held high and maintaining the posture of one who cannot easily be pushed down, stepped over or walked on when someone needs our help.

28. I am suggesting we make the meaning rather than trying to discern the mind of god.

29. Does this way of relating to humanity contribute to the prejudicial thinking that some people are better than others?

Constructing a God-Concept

should be a conditional act: it comes with an expectation of reciprocity.[30] Those who have nothing to give should not expect anything in return.[31]

The quintessential inquiry is to explore if it is possible to construct a *transformative* concept of god; that is, a god who would help me to think through the experience of losing my best friend (from a theological perspective), express how I am feeling so that I can develop empathy and become better adapted to help others and address contemporary social problems, e.g., poverty, inequality and global warming. I seek a god who will help me exercise my critical thinking, tweak previously acquired skills and develop new ones to become more socially conscious and socially responsible and equipped to inspire others to be and do likewise.[32] What if I could construct a concept of a god who facilitates this process (and does not need to control it), a god who believes in me and has faith in my skill set to help others, and supports me so that I can help myself and in so doing, learn how to help others?[33]

To search for a god beyond organized religion, I need to rule out that the god of organized religion is willing to accept the adaptive challenge of learning to do things differently (and the actual change may be limited to our concept of god). His choice of intervention is a technical fix: healing that which hurts, repairing that which is broken and mending that which is ripping apart at the seams. He wants to wave his magic wand and make wickedness wayward. His approach to helping mimics the archaic missionary methods of preaching to the poor that if they become penitent, provisions will be provided. Before he changes his behavior, he would have to discern a darn good reason why being "this kind of a god" (transactional) no longer works for him or the people who need him and rededicate

---

30. Those who cannot help themselves may not be in a position to be able to help others.

31. My contention is that this concept of god negatively impacts the way a society takes care of its poor. If the poor have nothing to contribute to society, why would we give anything to them?

32. Organized religion teaches people to be compassionate toward others. A higher level of teaching instructs people to help others to become more compassionate.

33. I began with the expectation it was possible to find a god beyond organized religion. It would be really nice to think there is such a god, even if that god has little interest in someone like me. I'm OK with that. It seems more likely a god created the universe, even if I don't have a "personal relationship" with that god. Even though the world doesn't always work the way that I think it should work, and really tragic things happen to really good people, there appears to be some kind of system, one of a higher order, a karmic balance allowing us to put in good to the universe and get some back.

The God Beyond Organized Religion

himself to learning a skill set to become "a new kind of god" (transformative). Truly, when one can say, "But I've always been like this" and you are an eternal being, it can't be very easy to change.

What if we construct a new or different concept of god, one which reaches beyond the previously constructed ones owned (the patent) and manufactured by conglomerates of religious organizations? Instead of sorting through the gods of global religions to choose a particular one, what if we imagine a god who reaches above and beyond organized religion, especially one which assists in the process of self-enlightenment, a process which helps me to identify what is within me that might be helpful to others? Will I be able to identify what I would need from a transformative god? I entertain the idea that this experience of loss may be an opportunity to rethink my concept of god independent of organized religion and that this process might give me the spiritual energy to grieve, the fortitude to integrate my new normal into the essence of who I am and the resilience to adapt to my new reality.[34]

On a fishing charter one day, a huge wave swooshed on the boat and swished me from the ship into the water. My life had been going reasonably well, managing psychosocial stressors and feeling a level of contentment. And what felt like seconds later, I was treading water in a sea of squiggly seaweed. Life had taught me to move my legs back and forth in a running motion to keep my body in a position of strength and security. Such skill served me well on land, but less so in water. Though not the most conducive situation to learn to do otherwise, I am now postured to use my arms in a new way, albeit awkward and out of my element. I give this some thought as my head bobbles upon the surf. I am tempted to plead to the god of organized religion, who stands on the deck ready to throw the life preserver, but I am already thrashing about my arms and legs in synchronic motion. I realize I can save myself and at the same time, learn how to swim.

---

34. The process can be described as A to B to C, not A to B and then beg the god to help me to return to A and pretend that B never happened. I do not want something good to arise out of something bad. Her death was bad and there is nothing that could happen that would justify covering up that experience. The quest is not "to get over it" and return to my old normal because I know, in my heart, I am not going to be the same person as I go forth.

CHAPTER 4

The "Why" Inquiry
Exploring the Options of God's Power

I never heard her lament the rhetorical litany "why me?" She refused to host a wine-drinking pity party where all the guests come to listen to a suffering peon whine about their condition in order to invoke sympathy from less-suffering peons. Instead, she walked into her future with her head held high; with courage and conviction that there was no reason why she had become one more casualty of cancer. She chalked up her fate to a combination of coincidence, genomics and environmental variables, instruments in the scientific symphony. When they are out of tune, they sound like finger nails scraping a chalk board. You just want to cover your ears and hope it will all go away. She resigned herself to her present reality, saying, "I can only make the best of the days I have left." The only reason to ask "why me?" is if one can imagine a spiteful, vindictive god who dishes out disasters and who would be willing to fess up and admit his involvement.

But I asked the question. I wanted to know why my best friend got cancer. I wanted to know why it had to be me to endure the emotional intensity of grief which felt like an anchor tied around my neck. I had to pull it behind me everywhere I went (to the gym, to the store, to work, etc.). I became a walking receptacle of pain. If anyone expressed an ounce of empathy, my pain poured forth as a flood of uncensored feeling. Like toothpaste, such a display of untainted sentiment could not be squeezed back into the tube. I felt as if a part of who I am had been stolen from me, captured by cancer and confiscated as collateral. A part of who I am had died with her and while I didn't want it back, it left a gaping hole somewhere deep within and now I felt empty and alone. Had I inspected the entrails of my emptiness, I would have felt my resentment which comes from seeing everyone else texting their best friends. "You can get a new one," were attempts at being supportive. "I don't want a new one," I retorted, "I want the old one back."

How did she happen to be one to get cancer? No offense intended to the masses, but there are a lot of other people walking around out there. Why her? Can her death/my loss be explained as some tangled twist of atomic arrangement, particles positioning themselves in a killer configuration called cancer? Was there a tectonic shift in the underground's titanium vault causing cancerous cells to invade and conquer her body? Did the clouds link up in an ominous formation with the stars in alignment, whilst the earth's rotational pull fell from the axis of angled aptness and astrological accuracy thus causing cancer to colonize in her carcass? Is it by pure chance, the coining coincidence of all coincidences that she would be the one to get cancer? Or, worse, was there a god in the heavens who set in motion a series of mitigating triggers which would eventually do harm to her? How can anyone believe in a good god who makes bad things happen to good people?

As my house was about to fall into the rushing water below, I stood upon the rooftop waiting for help and contemplating how quickly one's life can change. The "why me?" question is essentially unanswerable, its articulation is a liturgy of lingering longings, a catharsis of confessional creeds, an open door into places rarely visited, unlocking the most sacred wonderings of the soul. I propelled the query into cyber space to see if it would return to me in a meaning-making format. But the next thing I knew, the house collapsed and down I plunged into the raging river. In the stream of sorrow, all I could manage was to hold onto an olive branch moving in the same direction as the current was taking me. I had to learn to be OK with the seemingly endless drifting by positioning myself to go with the flow, to be prepared to shift body posture when the course curved and to develop dexterity for dealing with debris. Secure ground was out of sight.

The Why inquiry should only be investigated if one suspects god's hand is at the spigot, controlling the surge and able to damn up the gush before the water floods out an entire community and changes lives forever. He seems unaware of the effects of his actions. Does he not care about the impact by not plugging up the drain? Either god pushes the ground to create

The "Why" Inquiry

a mudslide or after the dirt starts to move, refrains from doing anything to stop the force of its destruction. Maybe he is powerless and stands back in total panic exclaiming, "Oh no, not the little children! Run quick. Get out of the way!" Does he ensure that the rich become more prosperous by leaking inside trading secrets or does he have trouble doing math and can't figure out why some people have more than enough while others are hungry and homeless? Either god makes people get cancer or god is not as powerful as is often presumed. There is no other explanation.

The "why" inquiry inspects the dilemma of divine power; that is, the extent to which a god has power to cause an event and/or intervene during and/or afterwards. The options of divine power include the following scenarios: (1) god makes events happen; (2) god lets events happen or designs the world with the foreknowledge of the unfolding potential; or (3) god cannot do a damn thing about anything, either by choice or submission. The first option assumes god has virtually unlimited power (by virtue of his authority as a figurehead and not because of social capital) and can access that power at any time or place. In the second option, god sits back in his easy chair and allows events to run their course. He may be too relaxed to care what is happening or he is trying to adapt to letting the peons do what he created them to do. He doesn't cause things to happen but tries to be helpful. The third option is that god has little or no power to stop global warming or save a dying baby or overturn political and economic oppression. Or maybe he moved away several millenniums ago and left no forwarding address.

The third option (working in reverse order) is that god does not cause bad things to happen to good people and cannot do anything about it when crises develop. This image is of a well-intentioned deity without the umph that a mighty god would customarily muster. He may not know which situations he should intervene and which situations he should let the peons do for themselves so he just tries to stay out of their way. He may not know what he should do which would be helpful because in the past, he tried to help but every time someone complained that he wasn't doing it right. So he gave up and said, "What the hell?" He's like a parent who throws his toddler over the boat into the water to teach him how to swim and while the child is thrashing about in horror, he's reading the latest issue of *Fishermen's Weekly*. Perhaps he had power but lost it in a card game with the other gods or got into a brawl which gave the winning god the power to rule over the peons.

The God Beyond Organized Religion

The second option is that god possesses limited amounts of power: either it has always been this way or at some point, he surrendered his "almighty-ness" in order to create creatures who would share power. Given this limitation, he can only intervene under a predetermined set of variables (undisclosed to the peons) stated in the heavenly bylaws. While this may frustrate him at times and hamper his style, it is in the contract he made when accepting the job of being god and he has to be willing to let go of some of his power so that the peons would be able to think for themselves, help each other and be free to make their own choices. He is quite pleased with himself when he sees them helping each other, yet at other times he sees the creatures making impulsive moves which hurt themselves and others and he hates that there isn't a darn thing he can do about it. He is bound by the pesky free-will clause in the covenantal constitution by which he must abide.

The first option proposes god is all powerful, an omnipotence that pervades all energy fields to cause and control the consequences of all events. God hyper-controls everything, every molecular movement, every dance of the Wu Li masters. He makes people get cancer (and he doesn't have to have a good reason or any reason because he doesn't answer to us). He is the possessor of greater power than can be conceivably imagined by the peons. He controls the direction the river flows and is the source of all things. He makes the butterfly flap her wings and intuitively migrate to Mexico for annual gatherings. He takes his crooked, decrepit finger and sticks it in a cloud configuration, doing a swirly which suctions the contents until they produce a destructive spiral, making a train-like sound with a force that can rip well-constructed homes off their foundations. He helps oil corporations get away with fracking in poor countries where people are helpless to stand up against them. He wants some people to be poor and others to be rich. He is the ultimate control freak and proud of it. There is no stopping him at the helm of the ship. He rules.

The Master Plan

He has a plan and he calls his plan "*the* master plan" (with an emphasis on "the").[1] Everything that happens was sketched out before the beginning of time. Everything that transpires happens exactly the way in which it was meant to happen. When a squirrel crosses the road but doesn't get across in

---

1. The master plan is based on the first option of divine power.

The "Why" Inquiry

time and a car squashes it; that was supposed to happen. Road-kill is a sign and serves some higher purpose for the welfare and functionality of the universe. Just as easily and without an ounce of regret, he can do the same thing with a small child. According to the master plan, he tweezed a tiny cancerous cell out of the Petri dish in his experimental lab and implanted it into her body with the insane intention of making her die. From the day of her birth, the plan was to let her develop significant relationships and then to snatch her like a wild beast pounces to catch its prey. (Anyone else who would devise these tragic events and think it in the best interests of society would be locked up tighter than a pickle jar.)

The master plan theology replies to the Why inquiry with the following conclusion: she was destined to get cancer. Before she was formed in the womb, god planned she would not die a natural death as an elderly woman, complete with wrinkles, crinkled skin and flabs of abdominal fat. She will never get to wear a moo-moo; half nightgown and half I don't know what. She will not watch her nephews and nieces get married and have children and babysit them, experiencing the complete joy of grandaunthood. God intended for her to suffer a horrible disease which would cause her pain as a prelude to her death. As her friends and family, we were destined to love her and lose her. That was the way it was supposed to be. And according to organized religion, if that doesn't make sense to any of us or serve some ostentatious objective unbeknownst to peon logic, then leave it alone or assign it to mystery but whatever you do, don't try to figure it out.

If there is a master plan, divinely inspired and implemented at every intersection and we have no influence as to which way we will move, then our lives are nothing more than a meaningless performance in puppetry, a senseless spectacle of marionette motion. God pulls the strings and we smile and dance as entertainment value for the other gods (both comic and tragic). Long ago, god set the keys on a player piano to record a melody that stirs and shakes us. God is at the wheel of his Tesla driving us to our destination. We are not sitting in the passenger seat enjoying the view or in the backseat directing his driving by yelling, "Slow down!" or, "Turn right!" Shoved in the trunk where our weeping cannot be heard over the alternative punk music blasting from his super-sized Bose speakers, all that happens is because that's the way he wants it. It's his way or the highway. Peons are like remote control cars; when he feels like ramming one into the wall or seeing how fast it can go until it flips over, so be it.

The God Beyond Organized Religion

The master plan theology presumes the god predetermines all events in the peon's life. The plan outlines birth and death[2] and diagrams in detail every event in between. The peons perceive they have critical thinking skills to make choices concerning the direction of their lives and what they will have for breakfast. But this is bogus. They perceive they are free to choose another peon as a life partner with whom to be there for each other through the tough and joyous times but this choice is an exercise in ersatz. Even though we might think we have some power to make decisions to fall in love, to discern our talents to contribute to society in meaningful ways and to decide whether we want to eat a cheese omelet or blueberry pancake, god has prearranged and preordered. The perception that peons possess critical thinking skills to determine vocational and occupational careers is preposterous.[3] The freedom to choose is a cinema in chimera.

One thing is for certain about the plan: it does not benefit everyone in equal measure. With the recent turn in the economy, the poor are getting poorer and the rich are getting richer. The poor are dependent upon their god for sustenance and the rich are dependent upon the poor to be willing to remain poor. Peons continue to dump carbon into the atmosphere with minimal concern for the next generation of peons. The icebergs are melting and the sea is rising. Some are victims of political oppression and lack freedom of movement, while others board their jet plane for a Sunday-afternoon cruise in the friendly skies. God doesn't seem to notice some people suffer greatly and experience an overwhelming amount of emotional pain. If we could see evidence that everyone got the same amount of good and bad in their lives and that everyone became more empathic as a result, then I could throw some support for the master plan. But "as is," the master plan doesn't demonstrate that this god is a god of justice.

---

2. A master plan presupposes our death is planned for a specific date, such as I am supposed to die on March 14, 2042.

3. Some have suggested that the peons get to initially choose (before they are born) which life they would want to live. A smorgasbord of spicy selections is presented to the life candidate who carefully inspects each and then chooses one. The life candidate is then implanted into the uterus of a peon to become a peon itself and live that peculiar peon-life. The problem with this theology is that some people live extremely difficult lives, filled with tragedy and suffering, heartache and emotional pain, agony and anguish. Yes, there may be moments of respite so renewing that make life worth living, but there are also those whose pain is never going to go away (until death). The idea that these people would have chosen to go through this because of some other perk or that they simply did not choose well seems unlikely.

The "Why" Inquiry

Perhaps the plan requires the sacrifice of a few peons, periodically and catastrophically, so that others attain something they need. A few bad things befall a few people in the best interests of having a few good things happen to the majority. Making a predestined amount of people die early in life is an attempt to solve the inevitable and oncoming problem of too many baby-boomers requiring medical services and too few medical personnel. A reduction in the number of people may address the problem of overpopulation (the god didn't anticipate so many people would want to have sex).[4] Perhaps knocking off a few people while they are young and healthy will warn the rest of us that we should do a better job taking care of ourselves, e.g., eating healthier and getting to the gym more often. But if all part of the master plan, then I guess it doesn't matter.[5]

What organized religion fails to realize is that the master plan and its purpose-driven (or non-purpose-driven) agenda overtly and subversively blame their god. If everything that happens, happens for a reason, then everything that happens, happens because their god is responsible. Adherents don't give god credit for the good stuff, preferring to assign accomplishments to their own abilities and talents (but perhaps thankful that their god created them with a particular skillset that enables them to get ahead.) When their god doesn't do what they want him to do, he becomes the target of people's anger and frustration. They expect something should unfold in a certain way and when it doesn't, something must be out of whack. Just about every bad decision can be made to look as if it was their god's fault. People are granted an outlet for not taking responsibility for their own behavior. What I don't understand is why organized religion insists we confess our sins and wrongdoings even if god made us commit them. Who should be held accountable?

If god makes someone drink to the point of intoxication, places him behind the wheel of a car and rams that car into another one, consequently killing the other driver, then god is to blame for all drunk-driving incidents. If god wants this person to suffer in order to teach him a lesson about driving and drinking, then this might do the trick (assuming he survives the accident) at the expense of the death of an innocent person not drinking

---

4. The world produces enough agricultural resources to feed everyone if we were better at sharing.

5. If my life is already mapped out, then I don't have to look both ways before crossing the street because I am not supposed to die yet (although perhaps not looking assures the master plan is carried out). I can be reckless and ruthless because "it's not my time to die."

and driving and only in the wrong place at the wrong time (or the right place at the right time according to the plan). Anything anyone does at anytime and anywhere is because that was how god wanted it to happen. Technically, the drunk driver could make the theological argument that they are not in need of psychosocial help but instead, need to be rescued from a predetermined set of circumstances (try explaining that to the state trooper to avoid a citation or a judge mandating court-ordered treatment).

The significance of such stringent strategic planning is that it leaves the peons helpless to determine their own destiny. Everything is laid out in succession and one simply shifts from one event to the next, with no forethought or reflection in-between. The master plan theology subtracts any opportunity for balancing frustration (with the direction of my life) with satisfaction (the hope of moving in a different direction) so as to motivate me to explore the alternatives from which to make a selection. If I am unhappy in my job, marriage or significant relationships, then tough noogies, because this is the way that things are supposed to be. I can readjust my expectations, develop better coping mechanisms and try to identify the positives even when I feel I am swimming in a sea of negativity. If I am miserable, emotionally disconnected, struggling to figure out who I am and what my potential is to become, I should succumb to the fate of my current circumstances. I am nothing more than a character in a Truman scene and all I can do is to play my role in the show.

The master plan theology reduces peons to pathetic creatures who do not control their own lives but often perceive that they do.[6] They travel to remote places, to spend time in reflection and meditation, and recount where they went wrong, the path not chosen well, to connect the dots, gain insight and realize why an event happened and how to prevent it from occurring again. They invest much energy into the "why" inquiry in order to feel some control of a situation and understand their involvement. They want to understand things about themselves and others so that they will grow and mature and become kinder and more compassionate. They think that they have a choice and sometimes they really believe the choices they make were worked out in their own minds and not enforced from above. In the end, we see all our decisions were illusionary thought-processes that were done so as to give us something of interest to think about. Our lives are basically mapped out from point A to point Z and every letter in-between.

---

6. Allegedly, this is the greatest of all sin.

The "Why" Inquiry

According to organized religion, the peons should realize their dependency upon god as the sole event planner. We are better off knowing we do not make choices; we are not in control of our lives and we are living out the sequences previously formatted to precise perfection. Sit back and let god rock the hammock as fast as slow, as high as low, as he wants to push. Push the button on the power recliner and watch the movie or soap opera series best-suited to his entertainment preferences. Passive positioning reduces the risk of resistance that might make one feel uncomfortable or disrupt the melodrama. It is futile to try to exercise any restraint to what god has in store or to veer to the right or to the left to explore an undesignated direction. We are totally reliant on god's prerecorded responses; that is what makes us peons and god, god. What life is about is adjusting our outlook to be aligned with the nature of the relationship between us and god; to accept our dependency and trust that everything works together for some higher good.

Organized religion likes to frequently say, "We don't need to know why god does what god does."[7] That is for god alone to know (perhaps for fear that if the peons questioned god it would be like questioning organized religion). If god wanted us to know, it would be glaringly evident and the curtain would lift and reveal all mysteries and secrets behind the scenes. As long as we believe in him, he will take care of us. Remaining in the dark with respect to purpose demonstrates to god our complete obedience to his will (or makes us look like absolute fools). There must be a purpose for not telling us about the purpose. I would be more likely to believe in this plan if I knew that someone else was going to benefit or that a pressing social problem would be solved by our submission. But thus far, I see no evidence that doing nothing makes room for letting god do a god-thing and solve these problems.

Excuse me for insisting that if there be a master plan, that that plan should have a rationale, a direction it is headed that should benefit someone or something.[8] It makes little sense to me why we would not be privy to

---

7. Organized religion has become the vehicle for submission to the master plan, weekly reminding the peons they should not resist the master plan and that it is in their best interests. However, when they see suffering in the world, they know the plan does not benefit everyone equally.

8. If the god knows us at all, I would think he would expect we would ponder his reasoning in the attempt to make sense of happenings so that we can learn from them. When we feel helpless, we can make sense of what is happening to us by using our critical thinking to find some strength to handle our emotions. We are, by nature, meaning-making

The God Beyond Organized Religion

that purpose so at least not to inadvertently sabotage its efforts and perhaps, even offer our support and lend a hand toward its fulfillment. Peons support that which they help create as every effective organizational development strategist knows. What makes the master plan difficult to accept is that it feels forced upon us by the big boys upstairs in upper management for the good of the company/universe. Such theology makes me feel even more like a peon and not a person. At the heart of any contemporary approach to a helping relationship, self-determination is a core value. God-determined in some pre-phase of existence denies me the human right to have some say about what I will do, where I will go, who I will be in relationship with, etc.

The master plan theology gets scarier when applied to our social and global problems. Is global warming all part of the plan? Should we do nothing, trusting that global warming is leading somewhere beneficial to the future of the planet? Or does the planet have a shelf life and global warming is a sign the end is near? In god we trust? Climate change, environmental contamination and global warming were prearranged to occur, along with human interference, to exacerbate the planet's demise. Recycling, repurposing and regifting are useless efforts to curtail the timing of this event. Eventually, the mechanism on the bomb, timed to the exact moment, will explode and the planet and everything that is on it will be reduced to tiny particles of deceased matter. There is nothing we can do to prevent this from happening, so we might as well continue to enable the process along. In fact, anything we do counter to the master plan (if we are able to counter the plan at all) may only prolong the inevitable.

He delights in the peon's quest to make meaning out of meaningless events.[9] He knows it's a waste of time but he wonders whether or not one of them will come up with some great idea that will help him figure out why sometimes he feels so out of control and madcap with all his power. When he is not on top of what is happening, he feels bad he didn't catch the problem in time and might have been able to do something helpful. Sometimes he knows what is going on but isn't sure what to do and so does nothing (for fear of doing the wrong thing and this is a recurring pattern). He regrets the occurrence of many events and realizes now that he might have acted

---

creatures who connect the dots so as to become enlightened and insightful. Thinking controls emotions and when we shift perspective or the way we see a situation, we can let go of feelings that gnaw on our self-esteem. Our great fear is not that a tragedy will happen to us or make us fall apart inside but we will not be able to make meaning from it.

9. Making meaning out of events is what helps the peons to readjust to life's circumstances and find strength in their suffering.

The "Why" Inquiry

to prevent them or reduce their impact and promises he will do a better job paying attention to what is going on. He likes that meaning-making is usually about him because he's god and the peons are just peons. He hopes that one day, one of the peons will figure out why he does what he does and how he might do things differently to get different results.

He resents that the peons don't take into account how overworked and understaffed is the hallowed office. In the days of organic religion, there were multiple gods and celestial toil could be more widely distributed according to skill and interest. The sun god took care of providing light for the earth and the fertility goddess facilitated reproduction and the water god provided rain for the food to grow. Postmodern culture shifted its paradigm to sift through probabilities for the existence of the god and the sorting out of the ones that could easily be replaced with scientific explanations. As fewer people today believe in fewer gods, heaven was forced to downsize staff. They laid off everyone who worked at the way station where people are purged to their final destination (figuring assessment could be done more efficiently with an app which calculates the amount of swearing weighed against how many good deeds were done). They did retain the devil guy because every team needs an advocate for an opposing perspective to anticipate resistance to change. The lesser gods now work per diem. He just wants everyone to know that it takes a lot of energy to try to keep things running smoothly in the universe and asks to be cut some slack when things don't go exactly as expected.

Perhaps the head god scheduled a conference to decide who would live and who would die this week. A chart is hung up for the lesser gods who need the visuals. The god announces he is not sleeping at night because the peons are so friggin' noisy. They hang out in bars and on the streets, partying to all hours and keeping him awake. If there were fewer of them, the cosmos would be a quieter place. It doesn't matter which ones are silenced by extinction as long as he gets some sleep. The divine council takes a vote (versus consensus building), their hands go up in response to the head god raising his, sealing the deal to send the fate fairy to indiscriminately sprinkle cancerous frost upon a few unsuspecting casualties. Just as probable, the god, the great god, the head honcho, the grand poobah, the master of the universe, the ruler of the righteous, the Most High Almighty and Exalted, points his crooked, decrepit finger at her picture and in an angry and vengeful voice, commands, "She must die. Make it happen!"[10]

10. He sits in front of the screen and watches what happens here on earth, pushing

The God Beyond Organized Religion

This god sits in his office with his feet on the table, wearing wing-tip shoes with tassels. He looks at them and wavers whether or not they match his socks. Mrs. God didn't do a particularly good job this morning laying out his clothes he concludes, because the brown and black argyle with blue background clashes with the brown shoes and the dark gray pants. He doesn't want anyone to notice this or think he can't think for himself and therefore incompetent and not to be trusted. He ponders this for only a moment because he's got other things to worry about: after all, ruling the world is not a stress-free job. Some of the investors are demanding miracles and he's not used to this kind of pressure. He holds up a picture of his family during their last ski vacation on Pluto. Checking his app for how many months, days and seconds he has left to retirement, his mind drifts to. He feels overwhelmed as he ponders the prayers of the peons. Their constant wanting and whining and wishing make his brain feel on overload.

He looks out the window from his office way above street level, as the hustle and bustle of the city down below moves with the robotic ease of precision. He is fully aware people are counting on him but sometimes he doesn't know what he should do and this predicament puzzles him. He doesn't want anyone to know he doesn't always know what to do for fear that those below him, either on the street or in the office building, will discontinue their admiration and adoration of him. He tries to put aside his own petty perennial problems to do what the company needs him to do so that they can promote their products. Like Johnny Carson, who behind the curtain may be a quivering mess of emotional insecurities but when someone announces, "Here's . . . God!" he pulls the curtain back and appears completely pulled together and is ready to serve. (I feel like Toto: I have pulled back the curtain to reveal that the god behind the curtain may not be as personal as organized religion would have us believe.)

If he summons you into the office and tells you that he's moving you to a different department, higher up, a promotion of sorts you may think he is doing this in your best interests because you have been faithful to the company. This transfer is nonnegotiable, irreversible and did I mention, in a different location. Besides, the people are nicer over there, they get a longer lunch break and the weather is seasonably warm year round. Suspiciously however, the guy who was doing your job before you came, suffered

---

the buttons on the controller to make people die or live (depending on whether it serves his purpose to reach the next level on the game). Having to push buttons got old so he devised a new system of speech-act in which now all he has to do is to say it and "it" happens.

The "Why" Inquiry

from mental exhaustion, went on medical leave and hasn't been seen since. Something in your gut gurgles but god gets to say things like, "I know what you need better than you know what you need because I'm god and you're not." You are to unconditionally accept that explanation because everyone else does and they do so because it is stated succinctly in the company's policy manual.

His attitude is that he should not have to explain his actions to the peons. They fall to their knees in the house of the rising sun and look up to the heavens and wail and whimper in anguish and agony, crying out for a reason why this is happening so that they can make some sense of it. He feels it is beneath him to have to respond. If he thinks it serves his kingdom then that should be good enough. He doesn't want to admit he accidently hit the wrong button before he drank his first cup of coffee this morning and a major section of the universe inadvertently exploded into smithereens, oops, whatever. He doesn't have to have a good reason for doing anything because he is not accountable to anyone or anything. "Hey, I'm god," he chimes when the bell tolls. One of the prerequisites for becoming god is that one has to full of oneself, greater than that which can be imagined and know how to tinker with one of those old-fashioned watches.[11]

If bad things happen for a reason and that reason is not immediately obvious or impossible for us to ascertain, what would be the reason for having a reason? If god has a darn good reason for making things happen to us but we are not made privy to what that darn good reason is, then what is the rational of having a darn good reason in the first place? When people say to me, "God must have a good reason for doing this," it is implied that we do not have access to that reason. Saying such however makes us start wondering what that reason might possibly be. But, for whatever reason, we are not supposed to know, nor try to figure it out. There is a good reason, god declares, but you aren't going to know what that good reason is (at least during your time on earth). The problem with this way of thinking is that having a reason actually helps people to deal with suffering. If I knew why she had to die, it might make it easier for me to deal with her death. Don't withhold an opportunity for me to make sense of it, let me decide that for myself.[12]

---

11. I don't know if there are any prerequisites for becoming god. Maybe he was just in the right place at the right time.

12. Perhaps I will not think the good reason is good enough.

Where I'm stuck is being able to conceive of *any* reason why the god would let her die. She had so much going for her: she was so full of life and love and laughter. I cannot think of any good reason to make her suffer with such a horrible condition as cancer, to go through all of the attempts to save her life and then in the end, not let her survive. Her suffering did not produce something worth going through. If it had to be done, why couldn't she have died sprawled out in her beach chair with a philosophy book in one hand and a watermelon wine cooler in the other? In the blink of an eye, she could have been transported to heaven effortlessly and painlessly. Why must the experience of death include the torture of one's physical physique? I cannot find a point to the suffering she endured. Why must so many people suffer in this world? What purpose does their suffering serve to them or others? I have seen extreme suffering that defies explanation.

Organized religion claims that the reason "why" god would pluck a blooming flower in the basking of its beautification or a person from the earth in the prime of life is because "he must need it/her more than you do."[13] God hosted a gotowebinar on succession planning and asked all participants to brainstorm about who they should get for this project and the only person who came to mind was one still enjoying life on earth. Yes, they conclude, she is the *only* person, living or dead, who can do what god and the company needs done. Perhaps there was something that she did here on earth or a unique aspect of her personality with which she was born that made her the premier candidate. She is essential to the team and so without even consulting with her whether she wants to do it, she was snatched from the loving arms of her family and friends and relocated to fulfill some heavenly task for the master. No angel assists her to negotiate an attractive severance package. If god needs us to do things on his behalf, one would think those things could happen here on earth in his apparent absence. In heaven, he can do his own dirty laundry.

A Theology of Behavior Modification

An alternative to the master plan is that god makes it up as he goes along. He does not map out the sequence of events from A to B and then B to C and so forth, but he is internally driven by external factors (e.g., crying peons). He keeps his fingers on the chess piece for fear he has made a

---

13. Not one of these popular sayings has any relationship to a particular religious tradition. They are imprinted in popular culture.

The "Why" Inquiry

wrong move and then as a split-second, last-minute maneuver with little forethought, moves the piece onto another positional placement. (When the devil moves his knight and captures his queen, he realizes he made the move way too impulsively and should have left it on the preceding square.) On the MMPI, he tested as intuitive and likes to show off his intuition in front of the other gods (rather than challenging them to a dual of fire like in the old days). He manifests symptoms of attention deficit disorder which makes him wonder if he missed his medication this morning. Sometimes he makes things up for no other reason than he felt like it.[14]

Or perhaps the good reason is a response to our behavior. If there is no master plan and god is making it up as he goes along, then possibly he is reacting to those peons who are behaving badly. His choice of intervention appears to be based on strategies from behavioral modification to persuade them (and those observing) to behave better (and heaven may be nothing more than a ime-out room). These techniques are formatted on this operating principle: if you behave according to the god-given commandments and the rules of organized religion, then you will be rewarded by having good things happen to you. Alternatively, if you behave badly by breaking any one or combination of those commandments and/or rules, then you will be punished by having bad things happen to you.[15] Both forms of intervention are examples of positive reinforcement (negative reinforcement withdraws something). Behavioral modification has been demonstrated to be highly effective as long as the subjects are pecking pigeons or salivating/drooling dogs.

When we poop where we are supposed to poop, god throws us a treat and we wag our tail in excitement to receive a well-deserved reward. All good things that happen to us are god's seal of approval we are doing a good job in the vocation of peon. In the school of life, are names are listed on the chart and every time we do something right, we get a red star. But those who take things that don't belong to them will become victims of tragic

14. Perhaps he lacks foresight to anticipate the implications of his actions or meant them for good and miscalculates that the consequences could so easily morph into natural disasters, personal tragedies and global hostilities. Perhaps there is a defect in the universal design: the genomics of creation predisposed to produce a pattern of imperfection that makes the peons vulnerable to victimization. Perhaps the god did not create a good world order from our perspective but works for him. Or maybe making us happy was not on his "to do" list when he woke up this morning.

15. Punishments come in the form of disease, natural disasters or situational/accidental crises; anything causing emotional pain, physical agony and/or spiritual aimlessness.

The God Beyond Organized Religion

circumstances (and there is no direct correlation between the nature of the crime and the punishment). Those who lie to their spouse/partner will be taught a lesson. Those who cheat and are jealous of others will be dished out a disaster. Whatever the bad behavior, the punishment is intended to prevent it from recurring.[16] With a hammer in his hand, he awaits the mole to pop up that justifies bang, bang, Maxwell. If bad things keep happening, one can make it stop by groveling with profuse pleading until the god backs off and lets the peon begin the humbling task of picking up the pieces of its broken life.[17]

To substantiate the hypothesis that there is a correlation between bad behavior and divine punishment, we would expect to observe occurrences when such behavior was followed by the principles of karmic retaliation.[18] As the robber is running out of the bank with a bag full of money clenched firmly in his hand thus raising his blood pressure in the thrill of the chase and the effort to reach the get-away car, he suffers a heart event and drops dead on the cement pavement. A businesswoman with no compassion calls in one employee after another to tell them that their services are no longer needed only to be let go a few hours later by someone higher up on the food chain. The person who holds up a sign judging the lifestyle of another arrives home to find someone standing on their front lawn with a sign judging them. If people were divinely punished after they did something wrong, then society wouldn't need a justice system because we could trust in the

---

16. Do two wrongs make a right? Should god respond with the very behavior he is trying to discourage? Do people change when they have done to them what they have done to others?

17. In this option, meaning-making is limited to figuring out what one is doing wrong so one can correct one's behavior; it does not facilitate the process of self-enlightenment because the goal is to return to a less functional state of health.

18. When some guy is lying in on the golf course because he got zapped by lightening, do his colleagues then turn to one another and say, "It was just a matter of time before god was going to strike him dead" and then get back in the golf cart and continue on with their game?

The "Why" Inquiry

justice of god.[19] We would see someone doing something really bad and expect that it is just a matter of time before they get what they deserve.[20]

And yet, that is not what we see happening. Instead we see the suffering of the kindest, most generous and compassionate people; the ones who pay for the groceries when the young woman in front of them has her credit card declined. Why is it that those who seem to be so willing to do for others seem to be the ones who suffer the most? I have known good people who experienced such tragedies that brought no truer meaning to the phrase "when it rains, it pours" and they did not own an umbrella. Likewise, though from a different angle, I have known frenemies who stabbed me in the back "just because" and went merrily on their way as if life were but a dream. Those who should get a taste of their own medicine so that they realize it tastes terrible are those who sip the sweetness of a stroke of fortune. Those who lack empathy and climb their way to the top of the jungle gym by pushing others off are the ones who get a huge salary raise and an office with a corner window.[21]

Her death has opened the dungeon door and released the dragon. I am angry.[22] I don't understand why this has happened to her (and collaterally to me). I don't know if I would feel less angry if I could see some evidence that those who do bad things have bad things happen to them because the compassionate side of my soul doesn't want bad things to happen to anyone. This world would be a different place if every time someone did something bad to someone else, others could see karmic justice play itself out, e.g., "an eye for an eye and a tooth for a tooth." Those who have a mean streak

---

19. We could also attribute such sequencing to bad luck, coincidence or factors by which people get into a situation fraught with potential friction. It seems unlikely however that someone, somewhere somehow would not be able to do some research to substantiate this hypothesis. If we could prove it, it would act as an effective deterrent for oppositional behavior. Everyone would know that if they do something bad (at least defined by the rules) the god is watching them and waiting to dish out retribution. Anyone willing to defy god would be constantly looking over their shoulder in anticipation of the ax falling.

20. If the sequence of doing bad and being divinely punished were not immediate, it would be ineffectual because it would be too long a time lag for people to make the connection.

21. OK so I am not making much of an argument for self-enlightenment as defined by selfless behavior, empathy and concern for others. Life seems to reinforce the opposite: selfishness gets people what they want.

22. If I could identify who has done this to her, then I could be angry at that person. I can't be angry at cancer as a collection of cells or whatever force is responsible for cancer.

The God Beyond Organized Religion

and just keep hurting others would have some horrible incident happen to them and everyone would know that that incident happened because of past behavior. Payback really would be a bitch because whatever bad actions one manifests as a negative force into the magnetic universe, would ricochet back to the same person with the same negative consequences.[23]

So how do we reconcile the observation that good behavior is not divinely rewarded and bad behavior is not divinely punished? How do we make sense of the null hypothesis, that too often, good people who do good things for others suffer terribly while others who do bad things seem to get off scoff free? Perhaps when something bad happens to the well-behaved, there is a glitch at mission control: the god fell asleep and while he wasn't paying attention the forces of bad obliterated the wrong person. Perhaps the god was on a staycation in the Bali Islands and ends up, the god on-call could not be trusted to follow the same rules of the game. Or possibly the universe was not designed under this code of justice (as organized religion presupposes), i.e., bad occurrences are not supposed to happen to those who act properly. Maybe the god never took a course in philosophy in college and wouldn't have passed if he had. I wonder if there is anyone up there who is keeping track of these things.

If there is such a link as organized religion proposes, their god should concede that it is an ineffectual one: people who behave badly usually continue to behave badly. Positive and negative reinforcements in combination with intensive counseling to gain insight into the impact of traumas of the past or emotive-cognitive therapy only change bad behavior when a person is highly motivated to do so. Behavior modification techniques often fail to make the necessary adjustments.[24] A good research consultant might

23. In defense of the devil, I do not think it likely that some guy is ruling over the underworld, traumatized by the experience of being rejected by the good guy, fired on the spot for his insubordination, kicked out of the heavenly manufacturing company, delegated to the bottom tier of management and to oversee those who can't perform to peak capacity. His problem is that his internal rage will not subside in time or be set free into the midst so that he can move forward and forgive and forget. He has to carry this rejection forever. He stands as a metaphor for what happens when we can't let go of the grief which threatens to consume us forever. I don't want to end up working for him so I will need to find ways to express my emotions, my anger about what has happened. Then, one day I will wake up and not feel as angry and begin to heal and move forward.

24. Perhaps this system is a work in progress and the god has not perfected the strategies needed to make it work effectively. Does the god implement a process of evaluating how well this works? If it is not working, can he reflect and admit to himself he has failed and needs to try something different before it is too late and we annihilate the planet with nuclear bombs and just wait for global warming to slowly but inevitably cook us in the

The "Why" Inquiry

be able to demonstrate that the modality could be tweaked to increase its effectiveness (presuming that the intended goal is good behavior). Those who do bad things and are punished (with more immediacy between the behavior and its consequences) might stop doing bad things in order to stop being punished by the god.[25]

When a bad episode befalls those who are trying to carry out the good in all their interactions, they often wonder and worry whether they are being punished for a lapse in prudence. The god must be punishing them for something they did wrong. They recount previous incidents of boorish blunders, prior improprieties in order to isolate the peccadillo prompting the predicament. Instead of devoting energy to learn new skills to adapt to life's challenges, they fixate on their former frolics. By identifying the culprit which caused the cataclysm, they cry for clemency and plead for pardon. In the midst of managing their suffering, they try to translate which trespass got them in this mess, committed as a transgression by commission or omission to make restitution and receive compensation. If they experience a respite from its secondary effects, they may assume amnesty has been awarded. They trust in a transactional god who exchanges repentance for reprieve.

In other instances, people behave badly, feel guilty about it but can't handle feeling guilty so arrange another situation in which to transfer their guilt. By doing something they know will make them feel guilty, they hope they will feel less guilty about the original event. For instance those who have been victims of sexual abuse in childhood (and experience feeling both guilt and shame) may orchestrate an event as an adult such as having an affair. They now have something new to feel guilty about (and hope that the old feelings will go away). Unfortunately, given that this attempt to alleviate guilt is an unconscious one, the second event tends to have a cumulative effect and they feel double guilt about both events. The mentally healthiest people in our society are those who do something they know is wrong and subsequently feel bad about it. Sadly, some people also feel bad about things for which they had no power/control/authority. Still others feel nothing and have no moral center. They are the dangerous ones.

Those who feel guilty tend to seek out a vindictive god who will assuage their guilt by metering out some form of punishment. When something bad

---

bio-atmosphere's crock pot?

25. People only change their behavior when they are in process of self-enlightenment and not because they are scared silly of a god with a mean streak.

happens to them, they can say, "God has punished me and now I no longer need to feel guilty." Traumatic tragedies become a kind of insurance policy that protects them from future guilt.[26] In the attempt to take matters into their own hands, some people will throw themselves over the cliff into the fire, as sacrificial payment for their bad behavior as if to make a good showing of their remorse. To demonstrate their sincerity to self-flagellation, they dive into self-destructive behavior by abusing drugs and/or alcohol. "I'll destroy my life before god has an opportunity to do so." They attempt to invoke divine sympathy so that the god will leave them alone. This way they can at least feel some control over their suffering. (What they do not take into account is that self-destructive behaviors usually impact other people, especially those who love them.)

Organized religion might actually cheer on these self-destructive behaviors by spouting on and on about a transactional god.[27] They can't stop talking about an angry god who executes punishment from a place of wrath and vengeance rather than concern and caring. (This god acts out of his own feelings rather than using those feelings to think through what would help the peon to behave in his own best interests.) Religious organizers act like the mother, who in frustration her children are not obeying, warns, "Wait till your father gets home." Father will not spare the rod. This outdated (and illegal) childhood admonition is supposed to whip us into submission to sustain the status quo. If you have done something bad or wrong or against contemporary cultural norms, when fatherly god returns from a busy day at the office running the universe: "Now you are going to

---

26. It is also possible that people punish themselves and then blame it on god. They feel unworthy and incompetent and they resign themselves to a less-than mindset (at least in comparison to others). If they retraced their actions back to other events, they would see the breadcrumbs unconsciously dropped along the way which led to their present circumstances.

27. E.g., If you do this for me, I'll do that for you and if you don't do this, I'll punish you.

get it."²⁸ Adherents become convinced god will punish them for everything they ever did wrong.²⁹ There seems to be no escape from his vengeance.³⁰

I would be remiss if I did not confront the violent nature of a god who physically or emotionally hurts people to get them to behave. Every state in the nation has enacted laws against violence toward another, e.g., childhood abuse, battering spouses and the elderly, hate crimes against those who are marginalized, etc. Assaulting anyone (for almost any reason) is deemed as bad behavior by the majority.³¹ Reacting with bad behavior to correct bad behavior as an intervention strategy must break some ethical code of divine conduct by the heavenly consistory. If god is trying to get people to behave by physically/emotionally hurting them, he is mirroring/modeling the very behavior he seeks to correct. He too should be held accountable. Anyone else who would intentionally smite an entire community because of the actions of a few or to save a precious few would be confined somewhere which would protect him (and the rest of us) from his irrational action.

Another leap in logic addresses what constitutes "good behavior" and who gets to decide the rules registering such actions.³² Power is controlled by the dominant group who use their money, prestige and connections to influence their own agenda, which not surprisingly, protects their self-interests above (and often at the expense of) others. According to the gospel of the rich, good behavior among the poor constitutes supporting an economy which depends on a set-point percentage of poverty and unemployment. In exchange for giving the poor just the minimum level not to revolt against

28. Those who construct such a concept of god easily become anxious and in their anxiety, go out and purchase armor to wear in case pieces of the sky start falling down upon them without warning.

29. They image god as the great father who now uses his IPAD to watch what is happening and doesn't even have to wait to get home because he can smite, strike or sting with one click ordering. Smiting is his choice of punishment. He used to obliterate whole populations but now prefers attacks on individuals given the cultural paradigm of individualism.

30. Some turn to organized religion (those who cannot afford the armor) as a kind of protector mother who will intercede on their behalf. To appeal to the god and curb its vengeance, they become a "super-worshipper" hoping that if they run away god will not be able to chase after them.

31. Some think there are some exceptions.

32. Throughout American history, from the beginning of its inception as a country, individuals have had the constitutional right to practice religious freedom. Ever since, organized religion has been empowered to decide the rules for what constitutes "good" behavior. Consequences for bad behavior are projected into the outer atmospheric cosmology (space) and to be instituted at the time of death.

the rich (i.e., public assistance), the poor are more willing to acquiesce. Yet, a motivational community organizer could gather the disenfranchised to protest the systemic inequalities and occupy a resistance movement, but he or she may be arrested for civil disobedience.[33] Good behavior, in the eyes of a few, may entail giving up one's seat on a public bus, being silent when the powerbrokers speak and subscribing passively to glaring inequalities.[34]

A theology of behavioral modification serves to justify the unequal distribution of wealth and supplies the fuel for the drive toward its accumulation. "If I have all this stuff and the god has given it to me, then I must be behaving within the limits." The rich applaud the inspirational speaker who frames their wealth as divinely allocated (and maybe god just wanted me to have it because he likes me better and not because I am behaving). Such theology assuages any guilt they feel as they are nudged periodically with pictures of poverty pervading this world.[35] When not feeling guilty and feeling pretty darn proud of themselves (and they may feel this way for evading god who did not find out what they had done; thus outsmarting a stupid god). They like to make statements such as "people create their own reality." From their high-rise perspective, people are poor because they failed to take advantage of the opportunities afforded them. While they publicly give god credit for their success, privately they attribute it to their own cunning expertise.

This theology also serves to alleviate anxiety among the rich about what it would be like if the tables were turned. What the wealthy fear most is becoming poor which is why they don't easily share what they have with others. This fear is wide and deep, especially for those who went from rags to riches. They invest almost all of their energy in becoming wealthy or preserving the wealth entrusted to them through a legacy fund. The money symbolizes that god loves them more than others and without a position of privilege, others wouldn't look up to them and their god wouldn't look favorably down upon them. As long as they don't do anything the poor would be likely to do (especially if they are generous), they will retain their

---

33. The god of the oppressed supports those who occupy in order to bring attention to the hoarding practices of big business.

34. Whatever theology we entertain to develop our concept of god, we must always ask the following questions: Who gets to select from the array of options and what is the criteria for selection? Who benefits by accepting one concept of god over another?

35. This may be nothing more than a commercial on television asking for help with feeding the poor in another country. They don't click over the commercial fast enough to avoid mentally registering the images.

station. "Nothing bad will happen to me as long as I hoard all my assets." As long as I keep doing what I am doing and think the way I am thinking, then everything will remain the same. Fear of being poor gets them out of bed in the morning and is the basis for almost all decision-making.

A theology of behavioral modification is so embedded in our society's collective (sub-) conscious that we assign it as an explanation to make sense of our contemporary social problems. For instance, when we hear about a person experiencing a crisis, we think, hmm, what must they have done? In that it is impossible to tell whether a tragedy is divinely-driven or a result of human error, the conclusion is that the person *must have done something*. This theology derives from a time when society blamed the victims of social problems, e.g., those living in poverty were lazy or lacked aptitude. Among the difference separating the rich from the poor, the level of access to currency is the most obvious. If a windfall of wealth was not viewed as a fate of fortune but a quirk of happenstance, we would perceive the poor in a different light. As long as we assign tragic consequence to individual behavior, we will arrive at similar conclusions to our social problems.

Behavioral modification theology may also generate a sense of entitlement among those who have lost something significant and perceive they deserve something of equal worth in return. Those who have been treated unfairly (by other people or by life's circumstances and/or by god) often feel owed some form of restitution which brought on their emotional pain (associated with the loss). They experience bad occurrences not because of anything they did or did not do (thus undeserved) and so feel cheated. It doesn't help when they look around them and everyone else seems to be getting more than they merit (especially among the wealthy). Their attitude is that the world owes them something (even if they cannot identify what that something might be). For the rest of us, we are caught off guard when someone who feels cheated out chooses to cash in and take something from someone else (and they think this will make them feel better or at least, less cheated).[36]

Whether one believes in the master plan or the behavioral modification program (and both run on the same app in that god decides who gets what), people tend to blame god for all the bad stuff. It is god's fault when my life doesn't go the way I want. If he is a good god who cares for the creatures he created, a god who is supposed to watch over us and protect

---

36. Our legal system is based on this premise. Lawyers promise their clients they will get them what they deserve.

The God Beyond Organized Religion

us from the evil forces lurking to inflict destruction upon the earth and its inhabitants, then he should be able to do a better job fighting on our behalf against the bad. A compassionate god has either failed miserably to measure up to my standards of entitlement to keep me from harm or he is an amorphous scapegoat whom I can blame when I set up a situation to get myself into trouble. It is convenient for the peons to have access to a target of culpability who cannot stick up for itself. Evidently, the great god in the heavens is not pulling his weight and living up to his reputation. And after everything I did to support him? I tried to do the right thing. I believed in him. I followed the commandments. Still, bad things befell me.

Is There Any Way to Convince God to Change the Plan or Withdraw the Punishment?

The question arises whether we can do anything to get god to change his mind (whether predetermined when we were an apple in our parents' eyes or earlier this morning). Are there scripted words that can be said to convince him to tweak the plan just enough to spare us from some upcoming tragedy? Is there something we can do to make restitution for our wrongs? If I am destined to have something bad happen to me, is there something that I can do today to prepare to cope? Can we bypass the plan? If we project god has all the power and we have none, then we are forced to bargain with him to change the master plan or back off from enforcing punishment.[37] Through the mechanism of prayer, it appears the god of organized religion is willing to barter to alleviate one's suffering. (Transactional gods are good for that.) Accordingly, organized religion works frantically tries to figure out what god wants so we can make an offering.

If there is nothing I can do to change my destiny and I am helpless to control its direction, then I am helpless to do anything to improve my life or the lives of others. I can do nothing to change my lot in life and therefore, I should accept that this is the way it is and nothing can be done about it. I should learn to be helpless as the precondition for a relationship with the god of organized religion. This god will help me leap frog over difficult circumstances and unfortunate events in exchange for my steadfast devotion and willingness to follow the game rules. He will help me to manage my dysfunction and the dysfunction of others by providing maintenance functions that foster feebleness. My boots are filled with cement and I cannot

---

37. We project our own power into the concept of god.

The "Why" Inquiry

move either to the right or to the left. My station in life is to be a miserable creature unable to make my own decisions and dependent upon the decisions god makes on my behalf. Infantilized, I crawl to the god who will cradle and coddle me.[38]

In his powerful presence, we feel like itty-bitty creatures begging for this or that, on our knees pleading for him to "please, please" modify the plan or withdraw the reinforcement. I am unclear how supplication actually works but it looks like the more begging the believer does (preferably within the religious organization to which one belongs) or the more sophisticated, theologically convoluted jargon the beggar uses, the more likely the request will be approved.[39] That seems a little irresponsible to me. I would think that a super-knowledgeable god should be able to make a watertight decision and if truly a sound one, not be swayed by the whining and wincing that gets him to change his mind. A wishy-washy god who can be hoodwinked, a sucker to the sensationalism of the demanding rather than the desolate and destitute, casts serious doubt concerning his competency. Like the wind that changes the course of its direction, for no reason other than because it can, this god panders to preserve his own popularity.

The predicament is to find a pathway of reprieve on the bad behavior-punishment sequence. In defense, organized religion has tried to conjure up with several fool proof means of penitence. There is the "god forgives you" so now you can go home and do it again but that implies it is god who has done the changing. Simply by saying, "I'm sorry and I promise never to do it again," seems to convince this god that the speaker has done the changing. (One would think that god would eventually figure out that his forgiveness may actually enable the behavior to continue and escalate.) When this individual exhibits the behavior again, the ritual of repentance is repeated. Some religious groups claim that their adherents are "saved" (from what I am not sure), granted permanent forgiveness and so others should also forgive them. This allows them to unmercifully steamroll over anybody and everybody because when they look back on those whom they have crushed on the concrete, they yell out while not slowing down at all, "I'm soooo sorry!"

Supposedly, this god feels compassion for those who do bad things and feels bad that he has to go through with the punishment. To be able to

---

38. Apparently, the god of organized religion has not heard the phrase, "no pain, no gain."

39. This is consistent with a theology of positive reinforcement.

The God Beyond Organized Religion

pass out the prizes, he has to also be willing to pass out the punishments. But if the peons pray exceedingly with extra effort and feel bad before the god feels bad, and promises, "I will never do it again," the punishment may be withdrawn or the master plan maneuvered.[40] What I question is the effectiveness of this intervention to encourage people to change the way they behave. How many times can we exhibit the same behavior and the god of organized religion will offer free forgiveness?[41] Doesn't he become like the abused spouse in this relationship whose forgiveness gives the perpetrator permission to continue to behave badly? Is that love? Have we confused dependency on god for love?

It's a neat godly trick because there are so many opportunities out there to get ourselves into trouble; temptations so tempting that it takes a lot of self-control not to transgress. And when we do, we feel a tension between that which we regret, what we feel bad about, a sense of shame and a desire to repeat the experience to get the same high. So we need a god who is a top-notch mechanic, a master of machinery, who interacts by breaking and fixing, breaking and fixing us until we fix no more.[42] When we get ourselves into a bad situation, we can call upon him (he's like the AAA guy) and he will restart our battery, fix our flat tire or tow us to another place if he doesn't have the right tools with him in the truck. In return, we either pay an annual fee and/or express feeling eternally grateful (whether or not god did something to sabotage the car is irrelevant). A transactional god drives this dependency; a dependency that makes us feel weak and helpless to change our own situation in life, much less the circumstances of others.

For some unknown reason, this god needs to be liked; more than liked, he desires to be worshipped, loved, adored, praised, set on a pedestal, idolized, glorified, magnified and more. He is willing to do whatever it takes to get the peons to profess their undying admiration for the almighty admiral. In exchange for people-pleasing the peons by answering their every petty prayer and petition, he expects them to gather once a week, in a location of their choice, to bring tribute and pay homage. To ensure this love-fest goes as planned, we beseech thee and he schleps in as the savior who wipes the slate clean, absolving with absolution and atoning with atonement. He is

---

40. The more appropriate word here is "godeuvered." I added it to my dictionary.

41. By free, I mean, all we have to do is ask for it.

42. In the industrial age, perceiving god as the master of the machinery made sense. If the god deviated from this concept in any obvious way, then something was wrong and needed fixing. In our contemporary conceptual age, we are more inclined to be drawn to leadership images of god.

The "Why" Inquiry

a shining knight on a white horse making a colorful entrance and we bow as he trots by. The trumpets blow, the ribbons swirl, the onlookers gaze in amazement, the triumphal entry of a god sitting upon the elephant's throne, looking quite pleased with himself. With a twizzle and a twist, he accepts our apology for all appalling actions.

The mystery is why some people get their prayers answered while others do not. Perhaps those whose prayers are answered are the biggest contributors to his organization or who have the potential to be wooed into this category if persuaded with presents. Perhaps god responds better to those who believe in him and so to keep their business, answers their prayers. Perhaps he feels obliged to service those with power and status or those with political clout and prestige so that their perception of him remains intact. What is the criterion with which he determines who gets their prayers answered? Are their variables to be isolated to make this determination as organized religion presupposes? What kind of a god would be swayed by such standards? How does it benefit the divine world to meet the needs of the rich, when to do so is at the expense of the poor?

He doesn't seem to give a hoot about some people, especially those who suffer from hunger, homelessness and hatred. He doesn't seem to realize that the present state of the economy has forced some good people to foreclose on their homes. His panoramic eyes don't seem to be able to turn wide enough to detect those who walk the streets to sell their bodies for drugs and who likely have been sexually abused as children. One might think the more severe the suffering, the more likely that a caring god would scoop up such a person with its beak and make a drop at a local rehab. Those who suffer with an illness, drug addiction or destructive patterns of behaving and relating seem to be among those least helped. If there really is a god who cares about being noticed and acclaimed, it would make more sense he would intervene in places where we see the greatest suffering. Instead, he seems to be monitoring the index at the New York stock exchange.

I understand that bad things are part of life: we wouldn't be able to appreciate the good if there wasn't an occasional bad slipped in for comparative purposes. I understand that the bad can motivate us to take on new challenges, adjust to compromise and develop empathy for others in similar situations. I understand that some cause their own suffering and "bring it upon themselves" and "pick up their first drink" but there are usually mitigating or precipitating factors which make people feel helpless and out of control. What I don't understand is how a good god can sit idly by on its branch and do nothing for a little child who cannot escape from a burning house. I don't understand how an all-powerful god does not act when a mother cries as she watches the death of her child as a result of starvation. I don't understand why a caring god doesn't help a desperate teenager who has been repeatedly bullied by bulldozing bigwigs and finally takes it upon herself to end her life and change her family's life forever.

If the world was fair, which technically, in a god-designed format you would think he could at least get that foundational principle to work properly, those who abuse dogs to express their victimization, would get caught, see the error of their ways and work toward full reconciliation. If the world was fair, dogs would be treated kindly and never abused. If the world was fair, people would at least treat other people with the same dignity with which they would treat a dog. If the world was fair, those who do bad things would be given some opportunity for self-enlightenment to realize the impact of their behavior on others.[43] If the world was fair, we would no longer need a justice system because what one does to others would revert back to oneself as cosmic karma. But the world is not fair and if the world is not fair, it is unlikely god is a god of justice. Once it appears evident that any god is not a god who doesn't embody justice, then we may question why the hell he has that job.

Not to run wildly through a mindless cornfield maze that does not get us to where we want to go, but I have one more peeve to put forth: "God never gives us more than we can handle."[44] Again, the blame for all happenings rests upon the shoulders of god (a theme consistent with organized religion's contradictory theology). God surveys the internal machinery of each person, their epigenetic, existential and experiential history, and determines the extent to which the mind can readjust and readapt to horrendous and haphazard tragedies. This assessment process predicts how we will respond and react to the trauma and its accompanying post-stress (secondary trauma). Pushed to the edge of the cliff, with toes clinching the unsettled pebbles, a few letting go and surrendering to the gravitational pull downward, god has figured out just how much we will take before we jump on our own accord. Sadly, and mistakenly in his error of judgment, some do.[45]

---

43. The concept of retaliation only promotes violence and continues the cycle of victimization.

44. If god never gives us more than we can handle, then why do we need god?

45. Such is the first step to taking the initiative and feeling in control, often following

The "Why" Inquiry

The counterargument (just so we are clear on the multiple perspectives here) is expressed through the following: if the god of organized religion never gave us more than we could handle, then we would never be challenged to do things differently, to learn from our experiences. "What doesn't kill us makes us stronger." If we choose not to jump off that cliff, we will become "stronger" people. While that may be true for some, it is not equally true for all. Some people do not jump but continue to suffer from mental health issues. Those who do not have enough food to eat and manage to scrape together something edible to get by the next few days do not become stronger as a result. Those who make the decision to walk away from a potentially destructive pattern only get stronger when they get help from other people so that they can help themselves. It is not the secondary gain of bad occurrences which make us stronger; it is the support of well-thought out help, based on empathy, which helps people feel healthy and strong after an experience of suffering.

---

an extensive period of time when one felt helpless. Death can seem preferable to the fear of death or the fear of always feeling this way and losing hope that one will eventually feel better. Perhaps it is not death which one seeks, but a way out from the clutches of a god who would allow one to get so close to the edge. If there be a time to swish, swoosh and scoop someone in their moment of utter desperation, this would be it. If the operating model says that god never gives people more than they can handle, then he has turned a blind eye upon those who seek relief from their suffering by taking their own lives.

CHAPTER 5

The Essence of "Me"

Her family did not wish to hold a formal funeral service in a religious organization (although her mother, a devout adherent, might have insisted upon it). Before getting cancer, she had warned me several times she did not want to be waked or memorialized in a religious organization and if I participated in such rituals, she would come back and haunt me. She was adamant no wake, no gawking at her, no comments that she looks so pretty and still so natural. So her family reserved a function room at her favorite restaurant where her friends and family could socialize, drink and mingle and recall their favorite memories of her with each other. There would be nothing "religious" per se. When the time seemed right to her family, I would stand before a crowd of people and deliver the eulogy.

    I arrive early to spend some time with her family before everyone else arrives. They are congregated in the back of the function room in a full circle, but when they see me, they create an opening inviting me into a place of great intimacy filled with heartache. When our eyes meet, they communicate something I cannot put into words, an emotional connection that makes us feel close to each other as we share the same sorrow. "I know," I mutter as I hug each one. They knew I knew. I understand what they are going through. I share in their experience of unbearable sadness which cuts through any protective façade revealing our true essence. If there be any comfort after losing my best friend, it is an emerging awareness that I do

The Essence of "Me"

not make this journey alone. I walk with others with whom I will grieve and laugh, mourn and dance.

After all embraces serve to sanctify this emotional connection, I saw her: she appeared right before me. It took my breath away and I gasped for air. Just as I was beginning to accept the reality that she had been obliterated from existence, she reappeared, looking straight in my direction. I realized I could see dead people. Confined to a frame, I recognized her profile picture from Facebook. She was standing in front of the water at her beach, smiling and she seemed so happy. The photograph sat on a table decorated with sea shells. Blue ribbons were attached to the shells so they were easily transported home. I suddenly remembered wearing a blue dress when I was the maid of honor in her wedding. I remembered the blue batik curtains she had made for the cottage and the ones she made for her house. The irony was not lost on me because I was feeling blue. I picked up the frame and held it lovingly in my hands, staring at her with an intensity of horror. OMG, this can't be happening!

I delivered the eulogy. I stood in front of a large crowd of people and began to speak. "She was my best friend for forty years" and started to cry. Once I start crying, there is no closing those flood gates. I cried through the whole thing, even as I managed to tell a few really funny stories. I felt a little embarrassed about my display of uncensored emotion, preferring a stoic stance which exudes a rock of resistance against the bubbling sentiment, percolating with pizzazz under the lid of the id. It's difficult to maintain one's dignified décor, collected composure, when clear mucous liquids are oozing from one's nostrils. When the levee breaks, there is no holding back the steady stream of tears. So I cried and cried and when I finished telling many of our favorite stories which we had recalled for each other countless times, I actually felt a little better. But in doing so, I had brought down the party. Everyone else was crying.

Her body was cremated and as of this writing, her family awaits the spring to spread her ashes. We will return to her spot on the beach where only a few months ago, she and I sat in our lounge chairs drinking watermelon wine coolers. We had walked along the shore of the ocean, letting our feet feel the coolness of the water and the mist of a breaking wave. I will stand at the very spot where I told her I wanted to write this book and be filled with sadness that she is not here to offer me her ideas and critique, her inspiration and creativity. We might have written about our adoration of the sun god who provides warmth or the sand god who produces every granular of grain. No sun god worship, no more walks on the beach, no one to talk with for hours about anything, everything and nothing.

I know she is still in existence. I am sure of that. I've realized she likes to play "Dream On" by Aerosmith (her favorite band) on the radio. I began to notice this was a recurring incident. When I finished writing the eulogy and got into the car, this song was playing on the radio. When I got into the car to drive home to attend the funeral, she played this song again. I can see her pressing the buttons on the heavenly jukebox. All of these incidents cannot be subscribed to coincidence and I have had enough of them to be convinced they are not my wish-fulfilling unconscious conning my rational thought. No doubt, she continues to "be" even if I don't yet understand the complexity of her form post-death or the function it fulfills. Somewhere out there in the great beyond, she still is, even if I can't see or talk to her. She may have climbed the stairway to heaven (she likes Led Zeppelin too) but she is not in some faraway place. I can feel her presence.

I wonder in what form she continues to exist. If she had her way, I don't think she would have wanted to take her body with her. Unless the existential program has an autocorrect feature to bring her body back before it got hacked by pancreatic cancer, she would be just as glad to leave it behind in ash form. From a metaphysical property premise, the body has a shelf-life. As it ages, it breaks and betrays and doesn't do so silently but with loud wailings to announce every oncoming ache and pain. What once could reach beyond its own limitations no longer has the same umph and languishes to retrieve its former glory. The impact of aging upon the physical body is distressing. She is never going to get old. She is never going to be a little old lady. Her skin is never going to wrinkle with little lines around her eyes and her hair is never going to turn gray. If she ages in heaven, it can't be in the same way as she would age as if she were still here on earth.[1]

If we have the option to take our bodies with us, then the god could simply tap the existential delete key and the body would be here one moment and gone the next. A family would be sitting around a hospital bed providing comfort to the one dying, staring blindly at a monitor recording med-tech data which they have no idea how to read. The dying one stops breathing and with the blink of an eye, the body suddenly disappears. The

---

1. I'm not going to tackle the question whether we age in the afterlife. I know parents who have lost a child will often count birthdays and say, "He would have been twelve today." They usually say this in the context as if he had continued to live upon this earth.

The Essence of "Me"

family notifies the med-personnel that their loved one has died.[2] But maybe no one noticed the dying person just got up to use the restroom. If I hadn't seen a friend for a long time, I may presume she died only to find out she took an extended vacation as a last-minute deal at a great price. Hmm, I don't think this would work. With a body in view, the family can confront the reality that their loved one has died.[3] We need to leave our body behind so our loved ones have a transitional object for the grieving process.

Even if our physical body does not arrive with us in the afterlife, I think it still likely that we retain our physical appearance (perhaps in the form of a hologram?). I guess I would prefer something which resembles me to being a blob of ghostly goo. If there were no resemblance to our earthly figure, we would all look exactly alike. (Let me put it this way: it would be worse than getting to a cocktail party and be wearing the same dress as someone else.) The idea that when we get to heaven we will all look alike (or like angels) stems from a prejudice that we are all the same underneath our skin. (In segregated societies, this misperception suppresses difference.) I want to look like me because who I am is reflected in my appearance (and my appearance reflects my cultural background). Besides, when I get to wherever I am going, I would hope to run into people who I know and be able to recognize them.[4]

Most religions believe the body is left behind while some aspect of the self moves on to another dimension designated as a "soul," "spirit" or "eternal flame."[5] Even though religions use different appellations, they agree it is what makes me "me." Its form is transparent but its function manifests itself so we can talk about what it does and how we can see it work.[6] I can access it during my lifetime but to do so doesn't seem to come naturally. If I engage in spiritual practices (not necessarily the same ones

2. In the real world, the med-personnel notify the family.

3. Too many families don't know if their loved one is alive or dead and it is the "not knowing" which can be agonizing.

4. I might be able to recognize them in other ways; but the primary way we recognize each other is by physical appearance. In heaven, we may need to develop better skills to recognize people beyond their physical appearance.

5. As a side note, I want to emphasize that I am not as anti-body as most religions. My body is part of who I am. This bilateral blob bore three children, ran seven marathons, has enjoyed eating a lot of good food, etc. I am neither ashamed of it nor repelled by its imperfections. Dismissing the body as nothing more than an "earthly tent" minimizes its significance in the formation of identity.

6. I will apply this same methodology to developing a concept of the god beyond organized religion.

The God Beyond Organized Religion

offered by organized religion), I am able access it. Discerning the nature of what makes me "me," how that form functions, the extent of its longevity (reaching beyond infinity) and its potential to achieve self-enlightenment will help us to encounter the god beyond organized religion.

Which aspect of what makes me "me" is left behind and which aspect goes to heaven is religion-specific. The following offer the four combinations from which each religion makes their selection: (1) the soul goes to heaven and the body remains on earth; (2) the soul and the body both go to heaven; (3) the body goes to heaven and the soul remains on earth; or (4) neither the soul nor the body goes to heaven. As I have already addressed the question about whether the body goes to heaven, I will now explore the nature of the soul which can be further subdivided: the occupational extract, the functional aspect and the organic essence, the spiritual aspect. By making this further division, we may be better able to answer the question, what part of "me" goes to heaven.

Our Occupational Extract

The occupational extract encompasses our psychosocial makeup: critical thinking, affective expression, coping strategies, almost anything which counseling seeks to tweak or improve. Tasks required for on the job performance include everything we need to eat, sleep, be loved, develop friendships, play video games, choose a life partner, find something meaningful to do while the body breathes, digests and expels. By its functional definition, the occupational extract is "transactional" in that it invests psychic energy for some measure of intrinsic incentive or extrinsic reward. Its favorite rap lyrics go something like this: "When I do such and such, I expect to get such and such in return." Mountain climbers expect to feel better doing strenuous exercise and take in a great view at the top. Those who go to work each day and do their job well, expect a promotion and more money. Those who sign up for an online dating service expect to find their soul mate. One puts energy into an endeavor with the hope of gaining something in return.

The occupational extract has only one customer: itself. Everything it does is to make itself feel good/positive/confident. Love, money and power are stepping stones into the garden of grandiosity. The god creates the creatures with an occupational extract which is self-centered and selfie-admired.[7] Narcissistic tendencies entice the occupational extract to do for

---

7. I did not acquire my selfishness. Therefore, it seems strange to suggest confessional

The Essence of "Me"

others so that others will like and comment on its own status and news feed. The paradox is that its sense of self-worth is dependent upon the perception of others: so much of what it does is to seek approval, acceptance and appreciation. Trying to impress and please others is its *Tour de France* as it desires to rise above everyone else. Arrogance is its middle name. The occupational extract is ultra-needy, high-maintenance and self-absorbed but its emotional dilemma is that it can't get no satisfaction.

The occupational extract operates under a compulsion to be selfish because it is constantly haunted by a fear factor: fear of rejection by others, fear of scarcity and fear of helplessness are the three witches stirring the brew and reciting the spell. These three fears consume the occupational extract with constant chatter about "what to do" to insure self-preservation and protection. Almost every decision is to avoid the anxiety arising from these three fears. By hoarding agricultural and financial resources, withholding affirmation (in the form of praise and other complements) from partners/spouses and not looking weak or vulnerable in any circumstance or for any reason, the occupational extract convinces itself it is in good space. These fears are so controlling they coerce the occupational extract to act with whatever means necessary to accumulate material items and emotional chips. No indicator light comes on to signal when "enough is enough."[8]

We should enter a judgment-free zone concerning the actions of the occupational extract. When it feels backed into a corner with no outlet, no way to escape, no window to crawl out of, it offers a warning growl before it either fights or flees or freezes so as to become emotionally bereft and empty of endurance. That which it cherishes the most is often that which it squeezes so tight, it suffocates the life out of it. Like a teddy bear which absorbs tears and frustrations, disappointments and discouragement, it becomes worn from worry and deflated by despair. The occupational extract does whatever it needs to do in order to survive; being authentic to its function. Therefore, we should not attach comparative value to the occupational extract (in relation to the organic essence). They do not need to compete for favorite status because both serve important functions interwoven into a cohesive whole which makes me "me."

---

rituals to acknowledge my selfishness as a sin or shortcoming. I would only do this to recognize my "need" for the god of organized religion.

8. The occupational extract is an emotional well which is never content or satisfied.

The God Beyond Organized Religion

Our Organic Essence

The other aspect of the soul, I will refer to as our "organic essence." This is the aspect which is eternal (has always been, is now and will always be) and has no transactional pursuit. Its function is to provide transformative assistance to achieve self-enlightenment (the perceptive process of discerning the inter-relatedness among all creatures). A support system of sorts, it works to manage the three fears by giving us courage to face life's challenges and traumas. Our organic essence energizes the occupational extract to connect the dots in situations which threaten to be our undoing and provides strength to take the high road when we would rather plot a painful payback. Our organic essence convinces our occupational extract to do the right thing (whatever that may be) because to do so will make us feel better and because being mindful of others' needs raises our consciousness concerning how we fit into the universal scheme. Whereas our organic essence is empathic (other-centered), our occupational extract is pathetic (self-centered). When my occupational extract shares the stage with my organic essence, it gives the former the emotional and critical thinking tools to explore who I am and who I am in relation to god.

Our organic essence cannot be contaminated by poisonous peons, nor polluted by toxic environmental chemicals or creaturely corruption. If it be a substance at all, it exists in pure form. It is virtually unaffected by life's calamities and accompanying emotional pain (which is so deeply and depressingly experienced by the occupational extract). The organic essence examines itself for the sole purpose of providing the most effective intervention to help the occupational extract become less narcissistic as one avenue to pursue self-enlightenment (the path toward happiness). Our organic essence functions to equip the occupational extract to be empathic toward the suffering of others. It feels to the extent it can identify with the occupational extract, reflect back emotions and help manage those feelings so that the "me" doesn't cross the line and become out of control (due to strong emotions such as rage, frustration or vengeful). Unlike our occupational extract, our organic essence is selfless and needs nothing in return for being helpful (transformative).

Our organic essence is generous toward others, shares its resources, expresses concern and comprehends that its own best interests depend on the interests of others.[9] When our organic essence sees people living in

---

9. The god beyond organized religion resides in the organic essence. It is not the

The Essence of "Me"

deplorable housing, it wants to volunteer for Habitat for Humanity and expend effort rehabbing and building homes domestically and internationally. When a house is burning and it hears a child calling out for help, it doesn't think twice about running in and retrieving the child in a heroic act of selflessness. When our organic essence hears someone else judge, criticize, put down or make fun of another, it stands its ground and confronts with compassion. Our organic essence sits in the balcony and makes observations while the occupational extract dances on the dance floor. It then returns to the floor to dance with the occupational extract modifying the way the occupational extract dances.[10] It longs to help the occupational extract to make meaning out of experiences and gain insight (knowledge) to practice affection (love) and encourage others to do likewise (empowerment).

When the occupational extract feels under attack by life's unfairness, it tends to put on protective armor, defense mechanisms which function as knights. The occupational extract locks up the organic essence like a mighty fortress and builds a moat, fills it with feisty alligators and hangs a metal lock-box containing a key on its massive wooden door.[11] In that our organic essence can be the voice of reason and the container of feeling, the only way to suppress emotion is to silence and restrain it. When the occupational extract is not ready to deal with a situation, all it can think is: how do I stop feeling this way? If only I could find a deserted island somewhere, anywhere, in the middle of nowhere, I could live out the rest of my life away from all my problems and everyone who is driving me crazy. But then it hears a faint whisper from the organic essence, who has managed to find a crack in the great stone wall, and offers words of wisdom so insightful and intriguing, one cannot help but ponder them. I can do this. I will get through this.

When a culture emphasizes the body above and beyond the organic essence, the occupational extract becomes hyper-focused on its physical appearance, sometimes at the expense of being able to access the organic essence. The occupational extract is aware of the organic essence, with signs

---

essence itself but that is where it feels most at home. It takes up residence in a place most hospitable to its presence. It does not need to be invoked, provoked or evoked to be helpful to me in my grief. It cannot be contained in a building, steeple, icon, symbol or scroll. The organic essence does not need to be accessed, cultivated or sanctified. The god beyond organized religion is present in all time and in all people.

10. Once one's occupational extract dances a new dance, others will emulate and want to dance the new dance too.

11. How to unlock this door is the subject of the next chapter.

of its presence and power popping up occasionally. The organic essence does not hide in the shadows nor does it need someone to turn up the volume. It does not want to draw attention or impose itself until the occupational extract asks for help. The organic essence has no judgment of the occupational extract; it is not sitting there judging every move but exists to be useful. Those who spend too much time focusing on the occupational extract at the expense of the organic essence are often the ones who end up divorced, diseased and disillusioned with this life. A healthy balance between these two aspects of what makes me "me" is imperative to walk the path toward self-enlightenment.

Are We Born Good or Bad?

The house of organized religion's theological tenets is built on the following foundation: we are created bad by god. We are born into this world as sinful, miserable and misguided creatures with one ambition and one ambition alone: to use whatever means necessary to satisfy the pursuit of our own narcissism. Lying and cheating are means to the end of satisfying these needs, wants and wishes, especially if to do so is perceived as the most viable course of action. Given our druthers, we would be nasty and mean to everyone with whom we interact socially. All relationships are nothing more than artificial adventures and commercial recreation. If we could make ourselves invisible, we would rob a bank and seek revenge on every person who has ever wronged us, revealing our true colors as spiteful, vile creatures. Others are avenues to getting where we want to go and once we get there, they are dispensable. Dishonesty, duplicity and deceit represent our inherent values (not by choice, but by design) f they entail exaggerating the ego. According to organized religion, we are bad to the bone.

Apparently, like money and a few cherished possessions, parents also pass along ancestral evil streaks, i.e., generationally generated badness. Immoral corruption and its contamination, or at least the tendency thereof or hitherto, is intertwined within the molecular structure of each DNA strand, to ensure continuance. All that is essentially "me" stinks to high heaven and I have my relatives to thank for the stench. I can be assured that I not only inherited sinfulness but I shall transfer it to my children (despite all my wise teaching about being kind to others and helping others when you are in a position to do so) and as much as I love them and want the best for them, I transmit wickedness (clinching the phrase, "wicked good"). Depravity and

The Essence of "Me"

mercilessness are our *modus operandi*, a condition or might I say, precondition, to existence. All that I am and all that I ever hope to become stems from an unscrupulous stirring, uncontrollable and uncontainable, just as it was for all those who went before me. Like hair color, weird tastes and peculiar expressions, badness is an inherited (genetic) trait.

Thus, we need a god to keep us on the straight and narrow. Enter stage right, organized religion helps us to manage these inherent tendencies toward errant, aberrant leanings. They teach that every baby is born with a chip of original transgression, since the very first human beings dwelt in paradise.[12] With no internal apparatus to keep us in line and inhibit awkward waywardness, we need someone or something to keep us from coloring outside the prescribed lines. On behalf of their god, organized religion functions as an external superego, the anal stick which retentively maintains an upright posture and a flat affect pose.[13] Organized religion helps us curb our coveting, control our cunning and contain our capriciousness. While we may resent such reprimand and resist such reproach, without organized religion everyone would run amuck.[14] The hand of organized religion is a strict disciplinarian and serves society by instilling fear so that creatures will consciously choose unnatural (that is, good and decent) behaviors of being.

We might wonder why a god would create creatures with a pinch of bad if he really wanted them to be good. The tension between being bad and the expectation of good behavior seems counterintuitive to an intelligent design. The core of who we are is in constant collision, desiring one thing but being required to do something else. Perhaps we are created from this mold to give bored gods something to do when there is nothing good on television. Bad creatures give good gods a reason for their own existence.[15] Perhaps we spice up an otherwise dreary day. If, however, it has

12. One could make the argument that placing a human being in paradise brings out the worst in them. Similarly, it is often noted that in the most tragic of human situations, something within people emerges that is truly remarkable: they are empathic, help each other out, and come together in more meaningful ways to work toward a common purpose/goal.

13. They accomplish this by teaching and reminding us what the rules are for good behavior.

14. Some say that organized religion helps creatures to tell the difference between right and wrong. This is not really an accurate depiction however. Organized religion knows we know the difference; just that we are more likely to choose the wrong if it meets our self-serving interests.

15. Organized religion has constructed a god who is all good. Everything he does,

The God Beyond Organized Religion

become tiresome to tend to the techniques of behavioral modification, the gods might reconsider a change in the plan. If god wants a better behaved creature, he should have done a better job with the architectural draft. We are simply behaving the way we were created and the god has no one to blame for this exhibition of error; it's his own fiasco. Yet, quite ironically, he still insists you've got to change your evil ways.

Therefore, we are born in need of being unbadded or debadded (and don't think I didn't need to click "ignore once" as I typed those words). Only a savior/deliverer/messiah can intercede to break the succession of badness. Organized religion has taken on that role or at least become the facilitator of its agency.[16] Their organizers are dispensers of exoneration and once redeemed, the adherent owes the organization (for the transaction of saving and amazing grace). The debt can never be fully paid; the interest is reduced by being affiliated with organized religion, but the principle never goes down. The balloon payment (directly payable to the god) is due at the time of death by recounting the good deeds done during one's lifetime. The reward is entrance into the heavenly arena above the clouds where those who need to feel above others, can do so for all eternity.

For those who have done wrong and feel bad, who are haunted by past behavior and have a workable conscience which functions empathically, they may turn to organized religion to assuage their guilt. An organization which funnels forgiveness may help those who know they have emotionally hurt someone whom they genuinely care about and are looking for ways to

---

he does is in the best interests of the creatures even if the creatures don't see it that way or share his enthusiasm. They cannot tolerate anything "bad" coming from the sacred world, perhaps because that would make them feel even more helpless in relation to him. If we are going to make him omnipotent so as to control the fate of the world as well as individuals, then we had better make sure that that power is pristine munificence and immune to malevolence.

16. Organized religion functions as a powerful superego, an internal source of control, often imaged as a parent figure that loves and cares about the peons and not wanting them to go too far and fall off the edge. This parent figure is constantly saying "no" and "don't do that or you will get hurt" and "if little Johnny's parents said that it was OK to jump off the Empire State Building, you think I should allow you?" An inner voice with a tape recorder of previous statements made by people who love us, to be replayed, reversed and replayed, may help those with a proclivity toward acting out (and harming others) to practice self-control. In that religious organizers serve as parental representatives, outlining the rules for good behavior and the consequences for bad, their voice is also deemed worthy of playback. They may say things like, "If you steal from your neighbor, you are going straight to hell" and if the person fears going to hell, they will not steal from their neighbor.

The Essence of "Me"

made amends. Organized religion offers them a way to begin the process of reconciliation. They don't need a rule-guru saying, "Thou shalt not do this or that," because they know the difference between right and wrong and when they do the wrong, they know it. Still, religious organizers will try to help them see where they went wrong, what they might have done to invoke god's punishment. Religious organizers try to motivate people not to act out, to refrain from imprudence and to stop whatever bad behavior they are doing at the moment (which feels good in the present but has consequences for the future). The premise of organized religion is to help those who have strayed from the straight and narrow to get back in line. Breaking bad becomes a weekly series of entertainment.[17]

My concern is whether organized religion, in its attempt to offer forgiveness to release people from feeling bad, actually enables bad behavior to continue.[18] If guilt makes people stop what they are doing (and guilt depends on empathy), then it stands to reason that keeping people guilty, keeps them from hurting others again.[19] As long as we feel guilty and express our intention "to never do that again," then the transaction is atonement. God's forgiveness deletes all our past indiscretions and wipes the slate clean of all our sins. But first we must confess everything we did wrong this past week so we demonstrate to god that we know what we did was wrong (even though we were fully aware that we were doing something wrong when we were doing it). Repentfully, we then receive a "get out of jail free" card which can be used in the future to repeat the ritual. (It's valid for about a week.) If one has plans for next weekend, one might take this into consideration: one might have to make the forgiveness last longer or see if there is a way to make it retroactive.[20]

---

17. In a typical gathering, religious organizers go on and on about our shabby subsistence and shoddy scum-like self. We are born bad and supposed to feel bad about acting bad (and there is no difference between being bad and doing bad). By cramming into the cranium how crummy we are at the core by getting in touch with the cheap chatter between ourselves and the god of organized religion, we appeal for mercy from god.

18. Religious organizers also attempt to keep these people out of religious organizations for fear that their sin will seep into the seats and saturate the setting.

19. I also question their interests as keeping people guilty keeps them hooked to the organization. If people really felt forgiven, they may no longer need organized religion.

20. The researcher in me says that if organized religion helps people to stay on the straight and narrow we could prove that with an experiment between a sample group of those who are administered a weekly dose of organized religion and measure their bad behavior correlated with a control group (and we would have to do our homework to establish a baseline between the two groups). We would expect that the sample group

The God Beyond Organized Religion

A theology of badly created creatures may also contribute to the social problem of prejudice and oppression.[21] Political regimes such as colonization and apartheid depend on a theology which justifies controlling and containing certain cultural groupings so that their "badness" does not disrupt the natural order of things. Left to their own devices, marginalized groups would manufacture additional badness on top of the badness with which they were born. Perceiving these groups in this light legitimates any mistreatment and malevolence. Given that they were "born this way" (although some may finish that sentence with "and can't help it"), those with political clout to determine their destiny perceive they are actually doing society a favor (so their badness won't seep out and saturate others). By constructing walls of division, politicians help these groups refrain from penetrating their impurity to the wider social milieu. (This thinking is so wrong on so many levels.)

Scientific methods have helped us to better understand that we are born into this world with an internal set of predispositions, neurological hotspots and genomic coding which act upon, interact with and react to environmental stimuli.[22] These internal proclivities make us vulnerable to certain frailties and challenges.[23] Our reactions are dependent upon

---

of adherents would be the ones who give all their money to the poor, walk a mile in someone else's shoes, reduce their dependence on fossil fuel, and inspire others to be more empathic and socially conscious. In the same kinds of situations the control group would be more selfish, while the sample group of adherents would be selfless. Their good behavior (and good attitude) would be attributed to organized religion so that others would flock into its doors, curious to find out what impetus they offer that makes others give away their resources.

21. This theology also supports the notion that some individual creatures are born with an extra dose of "badness," explaining why they act out and commit crimes and do really mean and disgusting acts, violating the human rights of others.

22. This contradicts the previously held notion that we are born *tabula rasa* (blank slate). Genomics has put an end to this theology. From a multicultural perspective, the theory is fraught with problems, not the least being the prejudicial thinking that "under the skin, everyone is the same" because the white middle class tend to think that everyone thinks and feels, they way they think and feel. If we are only the sum of our parts and not something more, then those parts are interchangeable and only add up to industrial thinking. We are not born alike and the goal of interpersonal interaction is not to get everyone to look alike and think alike. The god beyond organized religion creates diversity and is not on a melting pot mission to make us all one big glop of goo.

23. We are all born with certain neurological deficits (e.g., poor impulse control) but we are also born with personal talents such as artistic expression or the gift of gab. What might seem like a "bad" trait to one culture, e.g., aggressive tendencies, may serve another culture quite well, e.g., hunting. In the sandbox, these tendencies may constitute

adaptive skills acquired as an outcome of experience. In other words, we experience an event and develop patterns of reacting which are replayed in the next event. These patterns are a combination of internal and external factors (nature-nurture, e.g., the skills themselves are acquired through those around us who offer relational support). The interplay of these factors determines the available options for attitude, perception and behavior. Those behaviors form personal qualities, characteristics, skills and abilities. Each of us is a mixture of all that is good and not-so-good since our birth through the accumulation of our experiences.[24]

A significant difference between the god of organized religion and the god beyond is the "stuff" with which they create creatures. The god beyond organized religion does not create us as bad, as that would be counterproductive to developing empathy as the foundation for being able to help others and to work together to solve our social problems. The god beyond does not place us in difficult situations to make us stronger or to test us or to help us to appreciate the good (all middle-class ways of understanding suffering). This god does not create creatures as either good or bad, worse or better. Qualities or characteristics for such comparative and superlative values undermine the premise "we are all created equal in the eyes of god." (Seeing individuals, groups or whole nations as either "good" or "bad" is nothing more than a spoke in the wheel of oppression.) Equality is not achieved through the perception that we are all the same inside but by acknowledging our differences without assigning appraisal.[25]

The god beyond organized religion creates us with a tension between being selfish (the drive for survival) and being selfless (the drive for self-enlightenment). The tension between these two drives is constant, an active force in every movement, decision and outcome, a tug of rope between two polar opposites, pulling us in one direction over another, situation dependent. If one is hungry, one will use whatever means perceived as necessary to secure food for oneself, even if at the expense of being less empathic toward the hunger of others. At the same time, when one is eating, one might become painfully aware that there are others gathered in close proximity,

---

"bullying" but in another context, they may be the "stuff" of military leadership.

24. We are created with emotional and physical (basic) needs that the occupational extract works really hard to satisfy. When those needs are thwarted, when something or someone stands in between our occupational extract and its duty to be a good provider, it will do whatever it takes to break through.

25. Organized religion is often accused of its judgmental tendencies as it alludes to the badness in individuals, especially those who are unaffiliated.

The God Beyond Organized Religion

just as hungry, watching one eat and wondering if one is willing to share. One may feel some compassion to share but when one's stomach is craving nourishment it is difficult to achieve spiritual sanctity. And this tension is not limited to the security of food but almost every aspect of daily existence as we negotiate getting what we need with helping others get what they need.

We should not be judgmental toward the struggle between these two forces. Selfishness is not all bad and selflessness is not all good. What is potentially problematic is when an individual (or society) is impelled to either extreme: living a life of absolute selfishness, the accumulation of massive wealth with little or no regard for the basic needs of others or living a life of absolute selflessness, the giving up of all material possessions, going without one's basic needs.[26] Neither mode of living is productive because to evade life's challenges circumvents the process of self-enlightenment. Those who exercise too much selflessness, especially at the expense of their own needs (such as a mother for her child), burn out and frizzle away. "Put your own oxygen mask on before assisting others." Once one takes what one needs to be able to survive, then one should turn to see what others need because, ultimately, we are all in this together.

Each aspect of the soul serves as a strainer for these tensions. The occupational extract, the functional aspect of the soul, seeks self-preservation and determination. It cannot "be" without the sustenance of food, protection from the elements in the form of shelter and relational connectivity through which it feels loved and cared about. The organic essence desires to do good deeds and perform random acts of kindness. Yet, only loosely can one ascribe selfishness to the occupational extract and selflessness to the organic essence. They are not as conflicting in their missional aims as one might presuppose. In a spiritually healthy individual, they work together, a give and take of sorts, producing what I will refer to as "karmic balance." We are born with a genuine need to be helpful to others (a function of the organic essence and in so doing, we feel good about ourselves (a benefit to the occupational extract).

Karmic balance, the ability to manage the stress between being selfish and selfless, encourages the occupational extract and organic essence to interact. They are not entities meant to live separate lives. When one is disconnected from the other, individual and social problems ensue, which begs the question: how does a society help individuals to monitor their

---

26. This represents the difference between the have-gots and the have-nots.

The Essence of "Me"

selfishness and measure when enough is enough? Obesity of obsessive self-serving interests tips the scales in the opposite motion from the desire to be helpful to others. To plot on the continuum the tension between selfish and selfless, we seek to locate the spot where one feels the greatest ease between the poles (and the most at-risk position is when one leans too far in one direction and can no longer feel the stress of trying to manage both). Unhappiness, discontent and an abiding sense of emptiness and emotional void, is a direct consequence of being off kilter.[27]

When the music is suddenly turned off, the one who extends their hand motioning for another to take the only seat still available is practicing a selfless act of kindness. Even better is when two work side by side to advocate for more chairs in the game of life so that everyone has a place on which to sit. Pushing others out of the way for no other reason than to claim one's rightful place in this world makes others feel like losers and when they feel like losers they seek out less socially acceptable ways to feel like winners (and then everyone loses). Those who win are hyper-focused on the music and the chairs and the movement of the person in front of them while blocking the movement of the person behind them. Competition is the choice of interaction between people, groups and nations. We say "it's just a game" but most interactions between people in our society are based on competitive principles and competition is the lifeblood of our economic system.[28]

The Cost of Freedom

By design and designation, the god beyond organized religion shares power or rather delegates power to the creatures.[29] What the creatures do with that power is the cost of freedom. Some decisions will benefit the major-

---

27. It should be noted here that trauma can often pull one toward one pole and away from the other. When an individual suffers from a crisis, they tend to become more self-absorbed and self-centered. They feel as if they are the only ones who have ever felt this way and may become less capable of empathy for the plight of others. One of the most effective ways to help someone who has experienced a trauma is to help them to use this event to become more empathic toward the experiences of others rather than to focus exclusively on their own emotional pain.

28. Being competitive influences the way we experience god. If god is nothing more than a great parent, are we trying to get the god to be proud of us, to like us more than our siblings, to take better care of us?

29. I will address the timing of this designation of power at a later time.

ity with a cost to a select few, some will benefit a select few at the cost to the majority and some will eventually cost everyone (e.g., global warming). Very, very few decisions will benefit everyone. To change the criteria with which society makes decisions, we will need to change its core values *and* concept of god. Hopefully, the powerbrokers (our society's decision-makers) will use different measurement tools (other than a cost-benefit analysis). As long as we hold to a concept of a god who loves some more than others, we will make decisions which cost some and benefit others. An inclusive concept (this god loves everyone equally) will shift the paradigm with which we approach social problems.

If we are born as bad creatures, then we need encouragement to do good things or at least the motivation to do so.[30] Organized religion operates on this basic presupposition: if given the choice, we would choose the bad and need convincing to choose the good. Creatures are not wired to want to do good deeds or practice good behavior and so they need an organization to persuade them to move in a positive direction. Religious organizers try to inspire positive actions by threatening negative consequences, e.g., give money to the poor so that one will not go to hell or find oneself poor down the line. Behavioral modification techniques and tactics are what organized religion has to offer to society to inspire people to do good things. Twisting their arms only suppresses their internal drive to practice loving-kindness. Human beings however have an innate need to be helpful to other human beings. This is what produces the feeling of satisfaction when we successfully manage the stress between our selfish and selfless drives.

In a system of free will, where people are given the autonomy to make their own decisions, they will sometimes make bad choices and when they do not take responsibility for those choices, they may look around for someone else to blame. For some, everything that goes wrong has to be someone else's fault. They may be drawn to the god of organized religion who, maps out their life so detailed to cross every *t* and dot every *i* that one could make a coherent argument that god is to blame (for a flaw in the design plan). They tend to feel that everything is happening to them (rather than making things happen) and so go through life on autopilot waiting for the next crisis to occur. They accept their state of helplessness, as naively as

---

30. The dilemma is if this is an internal or external process: are we more likely to help others if we have an internal reason to do so or because someone tells us to do it (external)?

they accept their concept of god, because they perceive there is nothing that can be done to make things better. In the hole of helplessness, they do not need to take responsibility because they are not the ones controlling what is happening. The master plan theology gets them off the hook.

Pressure arises between the situations in which I am powerless and those which I have some power (e.g., to influence the outcome).[31] If I develop a medical problem related to obesity, then I might have exercised more and eaten healthier. If I choose to make a commitment to someone with whom I am "in love" but have not given the relationship time to be tried and tested and then I realize this person is not a good match for me, I might reflect upon how impulsively I make life-changing decisions. These situations are quite distinct from those who are walking down the street and are robbed, mugged, assaulted because "they were in the wrong place at the wrong time." Those who get certain diseases or illnesses may have not done a thing to contribute to the onset of their condition.[32] Some will be victims of other people's bad choices. There are things that we can control and have the power to impact (and are thus responsible) and things that will happen to us that are beyond our control. Knowing how to tell the difference moves us along on the path toward self-enlightenment.

What Makes Us Do Good Things?

We might also ask whether it matters why someone carries out an act of selflessness. Does it matter to the poor why people give them food to eat?

---

31. The process of self-enlightenment depends on our ability to identify which situations in which we have more power than we currently realize and then to figure out how to best access that power to help ourselves and/or help others to help themselves. The god beyond creates us with power to be helpful to other creatures. Accessing that power is what this god wants us to do, not feel weak and helpless and in need of divine rescuing. The process of self-enlightenment seeks to help us realize that we have access to that power through a number of different channels, including coming together with others so as 1 + 1 = 3 and creating synergy to make great things happen. First, we have to believe that we have access to that power. Second, we have to look for ways to go about accessing it so that we can do whatever is necessary to solve problems and create new solutions.

32. I can't think of a damn thing I did to end up losing my best friend to cancer. I do not think that the god beyond organized religion had anything to do with her getting cancer. It happened because of scientific, environmental, genomic factors that we do not yet fully understand. Our response is to fund research to try to isolate these factors and/or find a cure rather than wait for the answer to be heaven sent. Cancer deforms the health of cells and not a sign of punishment or a fulfillment of a master plan.

Does it matter to the environment whether people are recycling because they care about the future health of the planet or because if they don't and get caught they will get fined? Does it matter to those who are marginalized from the mainstream if people advocate for their inclusivity because they are empathic toward their suffering or because their religious organization takes up their cause and convinces their adherents they should do likewise? I suppose as long as the end result is a resolution to a contemporary social problem, or at least the beginning of a process to accomplish such we should be glad we are moving in a more productive direction. The end result is often our ultimate concern. But what I am demonstrating is that it is in the process of developing empathy that self-enlightenment occurs.[33]

The quality of help, the effectiveness to resolve our social problems in such a way that we are not putting a band aid on a bleeding body or merely suppressing symptomatic surface problems, depends on the extent to which empathy enters into our mindset. Too much help is offered in our society that is not helpful and indeed can be quite harmful when the motivating forces are exposed. Even those who are well intentioned but unaware of their own reasons for getting involved, can inadvertently do harm. Further, those who imagine what it is like to be someone else, do not necessarily guess right and may intervene in such a way that would be helpful only to those who are in the same social location and share a similar worldview. In such cases, the opportunity for a meaningful conversation (to develop empathy) may be a better way to figure out what the other person needs to help alleviate their condition of suffering. Our society does not provide a venue for such conversations and therefore, we are often at a loss about how to solve our social problems.

When it comes to helping another through a trauma, the emotional effects of suffering, one needs to be in touch with one's own emotional life. If one is too immersed in the selfish camp, one is likely less familiar with the selfless camp (only in the karmic balance can one improve one's emotional aptitude). The quality of the relationship matters. There is a big difference between someone who is compassionate because they are using their critical thinking skills to understand what it is like to be another versus someone who is trying to look compassionate because it is one of the rules for entrance into the kingdom and a ticket on the heavenly ride. In the

---

33. If all our social problems were solved tomorrow and individuals still did not engage in the process of self-enlightenment, it would be likely that we would create new social problems.

former, I want to be good and do good because being good infiltrates everything within me, cleanses me from the world's toxicity and helps me to sleep at night; it also makes me aware of the interconnectedness across all of creation. In the latter, I am self-consumed with pleasing the god so that the god will be generous when passing out favors. I want to be helped by someone who cares about me, not someone who is obsessed about whether they will get into heaven.

Since my best friend died of cancer, I have felt the most helped by those who have thought about what it would be like to lose their best friend to death. Some have tried to be helpful, connecting with me on an emotional level having lost their best friend too (or another significant relationship). They may assume I feel the same way that they feel because they have been through it. But just because someone has been through the same or a similar experience is no guarantee they will be empathic toward yours. Perhaps their best friend was high maintenance and a constantly needy and a whiny ogre and one is quite (secretly) relieved when death comes knocking. At the same time, because loss is such a prevalent experience in the human condition, one would assume everyone would know how it feels to be me and be able to relate accordingly. If you cannot imagine how I feel because you have forgotten what it was like when you went through a similar trauma, ask me. I will tell you.

CHAPTER 6

Divine Intervention
How Does the God Beyond Organized Religion Act in the World?

In her moment of desperation, when there were no options left to explore, she asked me to pray for her. The request made me cringe as I began to realize just how hopeless she felt. I thought it weird and out of character that she wanted me to go begging to the god of organized religion (or at least I assumed this was the god she was referring to). Feeling helpless, she was ready to be rescued from the rushing river, pulled out from the panicky pandemonium, salvaged from the sinking ship. She wasn't in the mood for self-enlightenment when her existential spirit was at risk of extinction. She didn't want to die. Any god appearing on the scene, regardless of form or function, who was willing to sustain her among the living, would have been a god to believe in and bow before. And when no god showed up to save her and death was imminent and the trauma inevitable and the loss irreversible, one wonders what do we have to do to get this god to do something? Do we have to jump up and down, yell and scream and then fall to the ground and pound our fists frantically, all while crying hysterically? What works to get god to act in the world?

I did not fulfill her dying request. It seemed senseless to supplicate to a god who would have already known she was dying and convince him to change his mind and let her live. Who am I to tell the god who rules the heavens and the earth, what to do and how to run his operation? If he

Divine Intervention

has any sensitivity toward creaturely vulnerability wouldn't he be able to surmise that we all desperately wanted her to live? Did we really have to fill him in? Is he that out of touch with the creatures and their suffering? To not turn to the god of organized religion as the god of last resort was a turning point for me: a conscious decision not to reach out to a transactional god who only answers the prayers of those who believe in him and who follow his rules.[1] I don't know if my praying would have made a difference in changing my attitude or perspective on the experience.[2] I sincerely doubt it. Still, something sitting in silence within me, feels an ounce of regret that I didn't go running back to the god of organized religion with my head down in submission, mumbling a prayer and moaning a petition.

Organized religion constructs a god who is transactional so that adherents can bargain with him for an act of goodwill, altering and adjusting his master (or morning) plan of action. If they offer a sufficient sacrifice (e.g., "I promise I will never do such and such again) they receive chips to cash in for divine favors.[3] Frugal peons will collect their chips until something big happens (or has the potential to occur) and then they have to calculate whether this situation is big enough to warrant giving them up onto god. Performing random acts of kindness, not stealing or cheating (especially when the opportunity presents itself) and worshipping this god generate religious capital so that one can approach the window between heaven and earth to collect what is due. That is the place where one comes to pray for what one wants above and beyond basic necessities. Kneeling with hands clasped together until they turn red from the pressure, one recites the cash-in-your-chips mantra: "I've done what you want. Now this is what I want you to do for me."

Maybe I am just throwing a hissy fit toward the god of organized religion because he didn't wave his wicked wand and make a miracle materialize. After all, if he felt like it, he could rescue all those who have no food and

---

1. For the record, I do believe in the god of organized religion, I just think he should approach the way he intervenes depending on the situation. For instance, when someone needs saving from death, he should perform a miracle, but when someone can do for themselves, he should not perform a miracle and circumvent their skill development. And I follow the basic rules for human decency and don't need religion to tell me how to behave.

2. What I don't want to hear from adherents of organized religion is that she died because I did not pray for her.

3. Holding on to the chips, keeping them in one's pocket is a superstitious practice when one believes in a lucky-charm god.

are held hostage in their own land. If he was so moved, he could push the delete button and undo climate change and its effects on wildlife, prevent all accidental spills and lick the oil off of every water-bird, pull the net off every dolphin and swerve every car before it hits a deer. If he wanted to, he could have prevented my best friend from getting cancer. I would be angry with god if I believed he could have done something but chose not to act. Worse, if I had been the one on my knees pleading with every ounce of fiber in my being for him to do something, anything, so that she would live and then nothing had happened, I would have hated him. With arms folded in a defensive position because he knows he screwed up, I would have confronted him: "After all I have done for you? When I wanted you to do something for me, you were nowhere to be found." And I am supposed to have a relationship with this god? That's not even how friends act toward each other.

The god of organized religion exchanges adherence to a religious organization for complying with all requests made, as long as set forth in the allotted time period and with sufficient entreat. (It appears to matter if one belongs to a particular fussy-cut container religion and has a personal relationship with the god associated with that organization.) When the god of organized religion doesn't act, it is because he won't (for whatever reason) given that he is all-powerful. As a mother pleads to save her daughter from being beaten, this god sits back, folds his arms and says, "I ain't doin' a damn thing." Maybe it's his day off and he doesn't feel like working. Maybe he doesn't like the woman or her daughter and sides with the perpetrator of the violence. Maybe the mother hasn't given enough money to the religious organization or missed one of the praise services or didn't pray hard enough or with sufficient sincerity. In my mind, there is no good explanation for an all-powerful god not to use that power when it could help someone here on earth.[4]

The criterion with which he decides whether or not to intervene is a little fuzzy. One might assume that he intervenes depending on the severity of the situation. An oncoming train plows toward a car which got pushed onto the tracks accidently by the driver behind him, a sniper about to take out a group of unsuspecting bystanders, a lost dog going through the trash looking for some morsels of food, all seem to be appropriate scenes for a

---

4. If there is a universal definition of sin, wouldn't this be it? I could have done something to help but I failed to act. Why doesn't that same philosophy apply to god's actions?

Divine Intervention

god to intervene. A young person who is about to die a tragic death, an advocate for human rights who is about to suffer horribly for what he believes in, a life about to change forever as a result of some terrible trauma all could be avoided if they met the criteria for miracle status. I have nothing against god performing a miracle; it's kind of a nice perk for an otherwise thankless job. I just don't understand why god goes to the casino and when someone is playing the slot machines, decides to use a limited supply of miracles at that moment.[5]

The god of organized religion intervenes in the world but he is a people pleaser and knows who the stakeholders are and caters to keep them content. (The illusion is that he works for everyone equally and cares about each of us with the same amount of compassion.) They pay his salary and he knows that if he can't keep them happy, he would be in jeopardy of being laid off and replaced by another god (one which would be even more loyal to the rich and powerful). Those who sit on the company's board of directors don't even have to ask, believe, behave, confess or plead: the god should know what they want without their even having to think of it. (They can hold to the theology that god will provide and that god knows what we need without even having to ask for it.) Their god is doing a good job when he can anticipate what these few people need before they even know. Showering them with surprising graces, his generosity is rewarded by getting to remain in the position of being god.[6]

The god beyond organized religion cannot act in this way and does not function as a go-to god for personal requests.[7] He is not sitting at a tech device waiting for someone to contact him.[8] He is not a personal assistant

---

5. I'm not sure where I am going with this: instead of more religious organizations, we need more casinos to witness to god's intervention in the world?

6. What god does with god's money is a mystery. If he gets paid by the rich to do good things for them then he should pass that money on to the poor.

7. The god of organized religion has it made in that he can perform miracles without any creature interference or involvement. He wants/needs the creatures to affirm these speech-acts. In exchange, he suggests the creatures witness to each other about these god-sightings so that others will believe, even if believing has no societal value without subsequent behavior. The god of organized religion also needs things from us but those things for the most part benefit himself (and not society). From the god perspective, we might wonder what would be the interests of a deity in being the "go-to guy" for every creaturely want and need? Why would a god want to hang out waiting for one of the creatures to realize a want and drop to its knees asking for a favor?

8. The god-geek, then, sits at the computer and does nothing all day but respond to emails with one hand, and text messages with the other (this god is good at multi-tasking).

The God Beyond Organized Religion

who seeks to serve. He is not an appliance repairman on call to fix something when it breaks. The god beyond did not create creatures as helpless. Instead, the design was set forth with a hope that the creatures would be able to help each other, even if that desire does not come easily or knowingly. Instead of waiting for the god to come to the rescue, to be the one to shine in the darkness, the god beyond envisioned a world where people would value their interconnectedness between and among all other living creatures and the environment and practice the principles of other-preservation in the interests of self-preservation. Instead of doing all the work to godage (see "manage") every facet of the functionality of the universe, this god's vision reveals the creatures helping each other.

The issue, then, is not whether the god beyond organized religion is all-powerful but the ways in which power is to be accessed, utilized and shared to promote the common good. Religious organizers tend to compress the choices of divine power into an either-or format: god is either all powerful or powerless (and as helpless as the people he seeks to serve).[9] They try to compress answers to theological questions to be consistent with that choice. They divide god and everything in the world (including the peons) into polar opposites as a ploy to sound persuasive and compete for right status. By making their god all-powerful, those who seek control of their situation may turn to him for assistance with the hope that he will use his power to help them in their powerlessness. Our approach has been and will continue to be to resist this tendency to talk about god with such excessive divergence. To move beyond split thinking, I seek to nurture the critical thinking skill of ambiguity: the ability to deal with the in-between, to tolerate the neither-nor and to accept the both-and; to embrace an approach which does not require us to neatly categorize the concepts of god into extremes.

Just as we are unaware of the extent of the power we have to solve social problems and help individuals deal with traumatic events (which are

---

If the god just took a break to get up and get a sandwich, he might look out the window and realize that those dark clouds are filled with acid. The god has debated several times wanting to quit this position because it gets old listening to the vast array of critical comments, underscored with moaning. Periodically, the god sends out a survey to see if it at all possible that there is one happy creature dwelling upon the earth who has something good to say about the created order. Maybe the god is just disgusted with our lack of willingness to take care of what we have been given and wants to walk away in disgust.

9. Very few religious organizers, however, believe god is powerless. The point is that they only see two options, both extreme ends of the continuum.

Divine Intervention

often precipitants to social problems), we project way too much (of our own) power onto god. An all-powerful god reduces us to peons who have no control over the course of our lives or to resolve our social problems. This concept of god promotes "learned helplessness" (enabled by organized religion) in which we do nothing because we don't perceive we can do anything. In la-la land, we sit back and talk about world events as if they are beyond our ability to change and we wonder when god is going to do something to fix the conflict. By depending on the god of organized religion as our "savior" who performs miracles and wave his magic wand, all we have to do is convince him to act. Prayer is an act of persuasion which attempts to get god to use his omnipotence to rescue, recover and resuscitate.

Different situations call for different approaches to power and dividing up power in different ways: (1) those in which we are totally helpless to do anything and we need a god to do for us; (2) those in which we could access power to help ourselves; (3) those in which we need god's help and power is shared; and (4) those in which neither god nor us are able to do anything about. There may be times when the creatures cannot help themselves and are powerless to change their situation. In that case, god can either do for them or teach them how to adapt to their powerlessness (and seek power in other ways). Not every situation should be changed. Self-enlightenment involves being able to tell the difference between these four scenarios.[10] Which situations do we encounter that we have no other choice other than to appeal to the power of the god beyond to help us? Which situations are we tempted to appeal for help yet we have the power to resolve on our own?

The Power of the God Beyond during the Design Phase of Creation

Before the world came into being, before the planets took shape and form, before conditions were conducive to support life, the god beyond organized religion designed how the universe would function; the principle of cause and effect, the capacity for compassion and the ecological pattern for the interrelatedness of all living things in the environment. The plan was to design a world in which people could find their own purpose for existence through vocation, craft (creating) and relationships. In the planning phase, the god

---

10. Whereas the god of organized religion is the target for change, the god beyond seeks to make a change in the creatures. We are the ones who must do the changing in order to change the world in which we live.

105

The God Beyond Organized Religion

accessed just enough power to complete this project (and perhaps distributed some power to other gods who were vital to its successful implementation). At this time, the divine realm had access to "all the power in the world" i.e., omnipotence, because there was not yet a creature with whom to share it. To set in motion a series of events which would produce life, the god beyond accessed only the amount of power that was needed to fulfill the vision.

When thinking creatures eventually evolved eons ago, the god beyond knew they could help with the process of creating the cosmos, a continual process of repurposing, reusing and recycling. The god beyond planned that the creatures would be created for the purpose of being creators themselves.[11] Therefore, the god beyond had to be willing to let go of some of the power at that time so that it would be available to the creatures. Once they had the capacity for intellectual thought and emotional intelligence and henceforth could solve problems on their own, the god beyond did not need as much power as it took to create the universe and essentially, returned some power to the reserve so that the creatures could access it and participate in the creating process. In this way, the god beyond models for the creatures that one should only take the amount of power that one needs to accomplish a mission or solve a social problem, no more, no less.[12]

If god creates us to participate in the power of creating, this implies the god thinks we are quite capable of managing and transforming the earth's affairs, from its global concerns to the traumas afflicting individuals. The theological indicator may not gauge whether we trust god but whether the god trusts us to do what is necessary to preserve the beauty of the earth and the dignity of every human being. The premise of our lives is what we can do to leave this planet in slightly better shape (rather than pressing harder to leave a deeper footprint).[13] Our contribution is not predetermined by some angelic consistory but based on our own observations, our ability to make an accurate assessment by viewing a situation from multiple perspectives and our willingness to collaborate with others. Best practices serve

---

11. Because the creatures are on the ground, they have a different perspective than someone on the balcony.

12. People tend to take more power than they need as a way of increasing their self-esteem and worth, e.g., to feel better about themselves. Because this is an ineffectual means toward that end, they never have enough. Whatever a society associates with power, e.g., money, is what people collect as a way to feel good.

13. If we are not created to do something that adds to the earth's preservation and its appreciative value (instead of subtracts), then the divine act of creating has a major methodological flaw.

Divine Intervention

the best interests of not one exclusive group which contributes money or time to a campaign to reelect the god of organized religion, but every living creature.[14]

I propose that the god beyond organized religion is not all powerful so as to part seas, cure cancer or make people fall in love. This god does not crash planes, harm little children or wipe out entire communities. The god beyond does not cause natural disasters such as hurricanes, tornadoes or floods. When insurance claims call these events "acts of god," they are talking about (and technically blaming) the god of organized religion. The god beyond does not instigate violence or fight wars or take sides in national, community or even family conflict. Either by contract and/or choice, this god does not control every molecular movement infiltrating the cosmos and its creatures and therefore, doesn't make bad things happen to good people. Creatures get cancer because of scientific and environmental factors we do not yet fully understand. Life traumas and crises will unfold, sometimes as a result of not-good choices made by the creatures themselves and sometimes just because life happens.

The god beyond organized religion cannot move mountains unless the creatures are on the other side, pushing and shoving with all their might. This god has no power to help creatures, unless the creatures are receptive to helping themselves. The god beyond cannot rescue, save, reconcile or heal without a human agent of change ready to act. If we are not in the mood to help another but have the capacity to do so, god cannot make us do anything beyond our readiness.[15] There are those who just don't care about other people or the environment (or themselves) and will hoard their selves as the best resource for being helpful.[16] The god beyond organized religion cannot be held accountable for what we do wrong nor the ways we hurt and neglect one another because we are the ones with the power to solve our social problems. This god refuses to enable dependency by which we invest our energy in pleading to the divine realm in lieu of problem-solving, consensus-building and community peacemaking.

Such a model of power and its allocation implies there are things that happen upon the earth and to the creatures which the god beyond can't

---

14. Thus, waiting for a god to come and do all the work because we whine and wail, averts and disavows the very essence of our existence.

15. A question arises as to whether the god beyond can act through us without our knowledge or willingness.

16. These are the people who can afford to send money to poor people in other nations and then feel they have done their part to alleviate world hunger.

do a darn thing about.[17] I can imagine it must be very frustrating when something tragic occurs and the creaturely covenant calls for collaborative support not sensational saving. There must be times when god regrets this arrangement, knowing full well that divine power could perform magnificent miracles or mesmerizing magic. It is difficult to equip someone to do something when we know how to perform it well and with precision. It is so much easier just to do it ourselves then to take the time to teach someone else how to do it. Seeing the big picture from up on high, I don't doubt that the god knows better than we do, but if all the decisions are made from above, and we make none, we may not support those decisions because we did not participate in the process. The god beyond must practice self-control to contain the desire to do for us that which we could learn to do for ourselves.

If the god beyond shares power and cannot act to answer our appeals, then how does this god act in the world? Does this infer that there really is no god (especially if we rule out the god of organized religion)? Isn't a god, by definition, a savior of sorts, someone or something who does for us that which we are unable or incapable of doing for ourselves? We presume there must be an identifiable line we can draw in the sand, delineating the competency of the creatures, the full range of skills, the extent to develop their adeptness to bring about social change, their talents to accomplish amazing and impressive feats and that which they will never be able to do. Should the gods locate that line and only act when the creatures reach it? Would the line change if they became more willing to learn how to work cooperatively together, to collaborate across racial/ethnic, national and political lines? As a species, are we on the path toward reaching our potential or has something gotten in our way?

By moving that line way to the left, this god realizes that the less it does for the creatures, the more they will do for themselves and for each other. The god beyond does not want to be the kind of god who subliminally encourages the creatures to feel infantile, helpless, out-of-control, dependent and weak. This god wants people to feel confident, purposeful and empowered. For the creatures to be able to help each other, they need to perceive they are able to do so and when they cannot do alone, to bring their skill sets together in a collaborate effort. An over-functioning god creates and sustains under-functioning creatures (as do religious organizers with respect to adherents) who perceive they need a god to do for them.

---

17. I am arguing that the god beyond does not have power to act in all situations.

Divine Intervention

The bigger the miracle, the more spectacular the fireworks display, the more astounding, astonishing and mind-blowing the marvel, the less likely the creatures will work together to solve the problems threatening global security and peace. We need a god whose vision is to equip the creatures to be all they are created to be.

There is a risk for a god who under-functions, who cannot perform the great miracles done by the god of organized religion: maybe the creatures will not believe there really is a god. If the god beyond doesn't wow us with wonders and if we don't need this god in the same ways that we need the god of organized religion, then maybe we will conclude, "There is no god." If this god doesn't do god-like functions, then no one will believe that the god beyond is a divinely-certified god. In response to this concern, the god beyond could care less whether or not the creatures believe, unless to do so motivates them to help each other (an assumption which has no apparent connection when studying the belief trends among adherents of organized religion). The god beyond is not worried about the creatures noticing divine intervention, preferring to be less visible, working behind the scenes and administering from the margins. The god beyond does not try to impress the creatures by being the center of attention.

And yet, the god beyond is active, energetic, dynamic and full of zip in the universe. While the god of organized religion doesn't need the creatures to perform pretentious acts, the god beyond acts through the creatures. The god beyond wants the creatures to look good, for this builds their confidence and capabilities (especially for empathy). Indirectly, creaturely success to solve social problems depends on their perception that they are created to participate in the functionality of every aspect of the workings of the world. The god beyond resides in the organic essence of individuals so they will take steps to alleviate each other's suffering and do something to save their environment. The god beyond organized religion is not in some far away, distant place we call the heavens, but within us. The god beyond acts through us so that we can make this world a more peaceful, generous and sustaining environment for all creatures.

Instead of praying to a transactional god to undo the consequences of climate change, this god acts through advocates to inspire others to reuse, recycle and repurpose objects previously deemed refuge and considered trash.[18] Instead of praying to a transactional god to send all that is needed

---

18. If the god beyond cannot act independently of the creatures, then there is no reason to pray to persuade this god to do this or that. The relationship one would have

The God Beyond Organized Religion

for the harvest, this god acts through organic farmers to teach agricultural advantages of nontoxic pesticides and teach another generation about the risk of overfishing to protect the barrier reef. Instead of praying to a transactional god to end violence against the oppressed, the battered and the abused (people and animals), this god helps us to identify the eco-economics of power and their accompanying psychosocial stressors. The god beyond organized religion does not act independently of the creatures.[19] Therefore, god is dependent upon us to stop global warming, oppression and all other injustices.[20]

How Does the God Beyond Organized Religion Act through the Creatures?

At this point in blogging about mind-boggling thoughts about god, a number of questions may be entering the forum. Can the god beyond organized religion act through us without our permission? Does this god infiltrate who we are only to take over, seizing the mind, reducing us to zombic followers? Does the god merely use our bodies to look like big things are done by small-minded creatures? Are all creaturely actions nothing more than divine interventions? What about those who have done some really bad things in this world? Was this too the work of the gods? How do we tell the difference between the acts of god through the creatures and the acts of the creatures attributed to the gods?

It is important to clarify that the act per se is not an action of the god beyond. The god motivates people to do good things but does not do the good things on the creature's behalf (good things creatures do would be nothing more than an illusion). If someone motivates me to do something, I might say, "I couldn't have done it without her," and really mean it, especially if this other person was instrumental to my being able to pull off the act. If god were physically acting through people, that would be micromanaging their behavior, and we are back to a master plan theology where

---

with the god beyond cannot be transactional for there is nothing this god can do for the creatures without the creature's participation in the process. The god beyond respects these boundaries and doesn't poke into people's business without their consent.

19. The god beyond organized religion can still act independently from the creatures and reserves some power to be able to do so. Unlike the god of organized religion, however, this is not the choice of intervention (for all the reasons cited above).

20. We are not dependent on the god as the god is dependent upon us. This role reversal is in direct opposition to the theology of organized religion.

Divine Intervention

the great god controls all behaviors, actions and events. The god beyond inspires us to do selfless acts, and only in this function, can we speak of god's form as "energy." It may be more succinct to think of this process as a sacred combination of divine and human working in sync to produce selfless acts of helping that could not be done without the other.

The occupational extract, by definition, is concerned about satisfying selfish desires and depends on the organic essence to help balance the two opposing drives. Others may call this selfless space within us by different designations, but that does not dismiss its definitiveness. (Some may perceive this to be a skill set of the creature, but I will discuss further on why it cannot be.) Our occupational extract does not need to be accessed; it functions on demand, e.g., when I want something and it is available for the taking, I go for it. We are by nature selfish and we all know people for whom being selfless does not come easy (or at all).[21] We don't know anyone who is completely selfless and does not exercise their selfishness (or they wouldn't eat). We need to discover ways to help nurture our capacity for selflessness. The question is how do we achieve this karmic balance between our selfish self and our selfless self? How do we access the selflessness contained in our organic essence and eagerly waiting to be utilized?

All of these questions revolve around one central question: what makes someone care? Evidently, some creatures care about our social problems and some creatures do not. Once we can observe such disparity, we can conclude that the creatures are not created to care. We are born with the capacity to be selfless (just as we are born with the tools to develop critical thinking skills) and thus to act because we care. So what we need to figure out is what makes someone wake up one day and care about others, enough to want to work for justice and to give of themselves for the greater good? What distinguishes someone's help that is crucial to the success of enacting social programs to restructure the systemic pitfalls of our society and those who don't show any interest in matters beyond their private sphere?[22] How do we go about nurturing that capacity to care?

---

21. Why doesn't the god just create us with the capacity for empathy, with an equal balance between selfishness and selflessness? It is because balancing selfishness and selflessness is situation-specific. Some situations call for more of one than the other. Critical thinking assists people in being able to gage that balance.

22. Well-meaning people work for justice but too often, they lack something and when this emptiness is examined, often turns out to be self-serving. (They have some self-serving motive for trying to be helpful.)

The God Beyond Organized Religion

Earlier I imaged our organic essence like a mighty fortress, protective of the trivialities of earthly existence and yet, locked up tight. Here, I will propose that the key to unlock the door is *empathy*. If you were to ask me, "What do you think god is like?" I would answer, "God is in the empathy." When people can imagine what it is like for another person or group of people, who can enter into their world and see things from their perspective and who can transport themselves to experience their experience, they are more likely to want to help *and* be more helpful. Empathy is critical to the process of thinking through what someone needs (when they cannot articulate it) by walking a mile in their shoes (or two) and feeling the way they are feeling. This is a highly evolved and sophisticated process and should not be taken lightly. Empathy is what helps us to make the shift from being selfish to being selfless; it drives people to access the energy/passion/enthusiasm to do what needs to be done to help alleviate the suffering of others.

This process begins with what I will call a "point of connection." This means that one identifies with the story of another. Those of you in readership-land may have identified with my story because you too have experienced a significant loss in your life. As I tell my story of losing my best friend, you are likely thinking about your story of losing your best friend or parent or spouse or child or colleague or pet. But I didn't just tell the story: I identified how I was feeling through the experience, revealing my emotional tone, expressing my affect. When I did so, you might have thought to yourself, "That's how I felt when I lost my best friend." Empathy connects two people or two groups of people as they find a point in which they have a similar feeling (even if the experience itself is different). That connection has a *spiritual quality* (are you with me?) in that it makes me feel emotionally close to another.

What makes someone "religious" is the extent to which they have nurtured their capacity for empathy. Therefore, one cannot be religious and lack the capacity for empathy.[23] This is a very different definition than the one set forth by organized religion (to believe in god and behave in accordance with his commandments). This definition of "religious" means that one cares about oneself in relate to others. Those who have been helpful to me, have asked themselves, "What must it be like to lose one's best friend of forty years?" and even if one hasn't had such an experience, to imagine

---

23. I would suggest we think of this polarity on a continuum. Empathy is on one end and narcissism on the other. Depending on where one falls on the line (and no one would be on one side or the other) is a better indicator of whether or not one is "religious."

Divine Intervention

what that experience would be like and respond accordingly. "That is so sad!"[24] When you respond with an emotional reflection, it makes me feel less alone in this world. I know you know how I feel because you have entered my emotional space and you are not afraid to feel the pain I feel and suffer with me. The god beyond organized religion is in this process.

I practice empathy when I consider what it will be like for a generation not yet born to be the victims of an environmental disaster caused by global warming. This makes me want to do selfless acts such as reduce my dependence on fossil fuel, recycle to the full extent possible and soften the indentation of my carbon footprint. I give money to the poor when I think about what it must be like to have nothing, to be pounding the pavement for a job and no one seems to be willing to hire me, perhaps because of my appearance or past history or lack of confidence or all of the above. I try to be empathic to those who have found themselves in no-win situations and made poor judgment calls on how to get out. I try not to be judgmental toward people who have strayed from their organic essence. Instead, I listen to their stories to find the places of healing and hope.

In thinking this through, she did receive divine help but I think that help came through me rather than independently from above.[25] I realize now I might have been helpful to her. In our conversations, I could hear in her voice that she felt some comfort talking to me, some momentary relief from her suffering, as I listened to her and imagined what it was like to be her and reflected back these feelings. Through my ability to be empathic, she did not feel so alone in her struggle and once I was willing to share in her emotional pain, to carry some of the burden, she had some respite from it. I learned that when we are willing to feel some of that emotional pain, we can provide a reprieve for the person experiencing it. While I cannot feel the physical pain she felt from the cancer, listening and being empathic connected us. Maybe she smiled every time she got a text from me, being transported to a place long ago and far away when life was easier.

---

24. As opposed to saying something perceived to be "religious": "God must need her more than you do."

25. I wanted her to receive the kind of help that would have miraculously cured her cancer or at least put it into remission. I admit, I wanted a fairy-god with a sparkly pink wand and when waved, make cancerous cells collapse. I wanted a lucky leprechaun with a pot of gold which could buy her a un-contamination kit. I wanted a genie who would grant three wishes, one of them being to restore her to health. With the exception of the tooth fairy wanting five bucks (is that still the going rate?) under one's pillow, the other imaginary pixies ask for nothing in return.

CHAPTER 7

The Purpose of Life, Death, and Dying

As I listened to her talk about her life and prepare for her death, she wrestled with deep theological questions. What is life all about? Why do we live and die? How should the creatures relate to other creatures and all of creation through this cycle?[1] If earth appears to be the only planet with a habitat favorable enough for the survival of human beings, are the gods experimenting before tweaking their design to be implemented on another planet? Does it make sense to create entire populations to dwell in misery and meander through mind-boggling mazes only to terminate their existence, exterminate them with a death-spray that stings? Why do some people who suffer not end up living so that they can at least look back on their suffering and assess the benefit exceeded the sacrifice?

A stroll through the woods, a run through a forest, a walk around a lake, a hike beside a river can nourish something within us that hungers for that *something more* to life. I spend my days on a computer in cubicle consciousness. Sometimes I take a break and look out the window and see the blanket of dirt that grounds the mud-making play box and wonder when the bell will ring announcing it is time for recess. The alarm goes off in the morning, an irritating sound that stuns the senses into awake status and then I let the dogs out and make my coffee. Tomorrow promises to be pretty much the same monotonous routine as today. If there really is such an entity as a soul in the traditional sense, mine has morphed into nonrecyclable

---

1. Creatures are created to care for the creation of the earth. Organized religion takes the opposite stance: creation is created to care for the creatures.

The Purpose of Life, Death, and Dying

plasticity. What I really want from this experience is to reconnect myself to a higher purpose, to discover meaning that makes me mindful to the struggles of others. For her death to mean something, I need to be willing to change something within me.[2]

I would like an explanation for our existence; some point of clarification about the purpose of transitioning from life to death and moving on to life again, a cyclical movement, a recycling of our organic essence. If there is no benefit to the creatures themselves, do the gods benefit in some way which is hidden from our vision? Are we nothing more than labor-intensive workers producing the fodder that feeds the gods? Are we the servants out in the field, planting, harvesting and planting once again so that our toil becomes their trade? Maybe I don't want to be at the beck and call of a god who says, "Jump," and I am supposed to ask, "How high?" There is no getting off this hamster wheel. You can't quit this job. There is no escape clause, no exit strategy, no way out of whatever reason there is for our existence. Even if one is miserable and decides to end one's life, the act only moves one to the next bus stop a little sooner. We are nothing more than peons in the grand scheme of what we hope is a grandeur scheme, a bigger picture that, when viewed at a distance, is supposed to makes sense.

And yet, as I think back about her life, I know she was an excellent nurse. Even after pursuing a number of different professional endeavors, she got to do what she loved and she knew she did it well. She once told me a story about a woman who was in the midst of transitioning from this life to the next, and the woman wanted to pray the rosary beads.[3] She didn't have any with her (and she would be the first to admit she didn't have any at home either). When I was visiting the Holy Land, I remembered this story and purchased her an olivewood set. As I handed them to her, she was a little bewildered, asking me, "What are these for?" but I reminded her of the story she had told me. From that time on, she carried those rosary beads with her in her uniform. I don't think they meant much to her (other than I had given them as a gift) but she cared about her patients, and she respected the strength their god gave to them (or their faith in god). She was there to provide whatever people needed and if praying the rosary beads works for some, so be it.

---

2. My basic premise is that we can change ourselves by changing our concept of god.

3. I am thinking this is nothing more than a superstitious ritual. The point here is that she would put aside her own religious thinking in order to help someone else and respect their religious beliefs.

The God Beyond Organized Religion

I can't understand why death has to be such a big secret. Why doesn't the god just tell us what will happen next?[4] How is it possible in all this time, after so many people have died, countless people throughout history, that not one of them has come back, even for just a few seconds, to tell us about their experience?[5] Is it that bad that if we knew what awaited us we would only go kicking and screaming? Or, alternatively, is it so wonderful that if we knew how great it is we would be like lemmings, rushing to the water to usher in a better life? Not knowing what happens next, we are like little children whose parents try to shelter them from too much information and in so doing, they guess worse than reality. We make up stories to cope with the not-knowing because the not-knowing can be harder to deal with than whatever happens. Here, I am willing to give the god beyond organized religion the benefit of the doubt that it is in our best interests not to be informed.[6]

When I was a child, I prayed every night that my parents would never die. "Please god, let my parents live forever."[7] What if we were offered an opportunity to live our eternal existence here on earth? What would it be like to live forever and ever? Would we live our lives differently if the deliverer of death was let go from her heavenly duties? Her lips curled, she is ever ready to snuff out our life-sustaining flame, to smother our breathing and to douse us into death. What would life be like if we could not die? Like a cartoon character after being squashed flat by the roadrunner, we shake and our body reconfigures to its original form. Like a balloon that gets punctured, a little chewing gum covers the air hole, and we are good to go. Subtract death and there would be no reason to look both ways before crossing the street, because if a car hit me, it would bounce off me like a bumper amusement. No one would worry about drinking too much and getting behind the wheel of a car because it would be impossible to kill

---

4. Maybe the god doesn't know what comes next and is only the god of this life, this planet and when we pass into death, another god takes over.

5. Several people have written stories about near-death experiences and even about the afterlife. What we would want to pay attention to would be similarities or themes interweaving their stories.

6. Such information may help us to alleviate some anxiety and the god beyond organized religion prefers to help us to manage our anxiety and sense of helplessness in the process of self-enlightenment.

7. I'm not sure my parents would have any interest in living this lifetime for all eternity.

The Purpose of Life, Death, and Dying

anyone.[8] Pancreatic cancer would have no power and retreat whimpering in defeat.

If all other living creatures continued to participate in the life-cycle program, being born anew in its season, human creatures might feel disconnected from their ecological environment. They may become envious of the living-dying, as the ebb and flow generates momentum and spiritual energy, while they feel stuck in the swamp of stagnancy, freaking out in a funk. As global warming grouts the breathable surfaces, the human creatures will likely outlive this planet. The ecological abuse it has suffered will wear thin and the human creatures will become homeless or rather planet-less and set a drift into the astronomical atmosphere in hope of coming upon a gravitational pull to ground us again. With a twinge of regret we didn't act sooner to set policies against the emission of greenhouse gases, presuming advocates to be shame soothsayers, now we wish we had done things differently as we float frenetically. Eternal drifting will seem like an awful long time.

Babies would no longer be born (unless the factory failed to get the memo and continued mass producing human creatures further contributing to the global problem of overpopulation). There would be no need to replenish the supply if there were no demand due to death. Evolution may erase the desire for the reproductive act because that which loses its meaning tends to lose its motivation. The concepts of physical maturity, emotional aptitude and self-enlightenment would no longer be used in everyday language. Without a continual matriculation of energy, life would not be a slide show but a freeze frame. A flower would always be in bloom, a tree would always have leaves and the grass would always be green.[9] Nothing would really matter because nothing would change; everything would be the same as it was yesterday, is today and will be tomorrow.

A contradiction may arise if our bodies continued to become weak and frail, feeling the effects of the aging process. By the age of 100, most people feel challenged to be able to do the same physical activities they have enjoyed and which give them a sense of purpose, value and independence. What would it be like if they had to rough it out for another hundred years? What would they feel like by the age of 200? Most of us are worried about

---

8. I suppose we could still physically hurt each other, just not die. If we could not physically hurt each other, it would be interesting to speculate as to how that would impact war, bullying, physical/sexual abuse, spouse and elder battering, etc.

9. A flower would never bloom, a tree would never have leaves and the grass would never be green.

The God Beyond Organized Religion

not being able to take care of ourselves, being a burden to our families who will feel obligated when we reach that time in life when we are unable to take care of ourselves. Thank goodness, that phase of life doesn't last long. As I approach middle age, I am already sensing things are not working as efficiently as they were in my youth. I'm worried about how I am going to look and feel at 60 never mind 160.[10] I wouldn't think anyone would want to live forever if the body aged at the same rate of deterioration.[11]

Or we could live forever and stop the aging process at the push of a (belly) button or get to old age, think back on what we perceived to be the perfect age and then be freeze-framed. Once one pushed the button, one would never by any physically different.[12] That would be a tough decision, as I know myself, I would likely regret whatever age I choose and eventually want to change my mind. No, it would be locked in for all eternity. (I suppose they could make it so that one could be a specific age for a designated time and then push the button again.[13]) To make an informed decision, I would think one would have to experience a lifetime and then make their eternal-age selection. The risk may be that we would have a society of young people if everyone chose an age under thirty-five (really?). I don't think I would want to relive those early years as they had their challenges too. The changing years, the aging process is all part of the creaturely experience.

Another option is that every living creature matured but reached a certain stage of life and then instead of continuing to age, "de-aged" in the opposite direction. When someone gave their age, say, "I am forty-two," the next question would be "Which way?" (This would be a question someone asks on a dating site.) I might be headed back to being an infant (and in this new system there would have to be someone headed in the opposite direction so that they could take care of me). Or we move back and forth over a decade or a developmental phase, e.g., adolescence, so as not to be bored. The elder years may dissipate from the landscape and there would be no more grandmotherly types around to be those nurturing, stable figures

---

10. Maybe the god could create us so that we age at a slower pace. Only after several decades would someone note, "There seems to be something different about you. Did you change your hair style?"

11. Maybe we could find a way to slow down the aging process. Over a decade, the total effects of aging would be barely noticeable and it would take several hundred years before someone would notice another wrinkle.

12. If that the body did not age, could the mind still mature in its capacity for critical thought.

13. Or maybe one just decides each morning what age one feels like being today.

The Purpose of Life, Death, and Dying

for the rest of us. Family dynamics would take on a whole new set of issues and potential dysfunction, especially when no one feels like being the parent that week to set limits on all the teenagers in the house and everyone is doing his or her own thing and nothing is getting done.

Then there would be the issue of time in our fantasy animation of eternal existence here on earth. If there were no such thing as death and we lived forever, time would not only *seem* forever, it would in *actuality* go on forever. There would be almost no sense of urgency to get something accomplished because one really would have all the time in the world. College students in every university would dance for joy because when someone says, "Don't put off till tomorrow what you can do today," that phrase would be meaningless (and they would point this out). In the new order, one doesn't have to do anything today if one doesn't feel like it. Hopefully, one will feel like it tomorrow or after one retakes the course because one failed it the first time around. No big deal (unless parents have to repay for the course) if we are not in the mood to study for an exam or write a paper or even attend class. We really can do it tomorrow. Practicing procrastination and squandering opportunities for advancement would be commonplace.[14]

I would not want to extend my time hanging out in an assisted living facility where a young woman is employed to turn my hair back to its original color. Every day I will go to water aerobics and wear a water-suspension belt and sit on a Styrofoam tube so that my body stays afloat. I will become painfully aware of how dependent I am on other people for my care and reality will mock me when I look in the mirror. Even though I will feel as though I am still in my forties, the reflection will be of a much older woman. Eventually the time will come when I am no longer ambulatory and I will be confined to a bed, where painful sores and unanticipated bodily discharges will fill my waking concerns. The day will arrive when my family members will gather around the bed and watch every breath I take to monitor whether I am still among the living. They will sense the ambivalence I feel, "Should I go or should I stay?" The goddess morphemes

---

14. The accumulation of wealth would certainly take on new dimensions as there would be no inheritance laws because people would never give up their money and they would continue to invest and never let go of it. The rich would become richer and the poor would never have a chance to get any money because the wealthy never die. Our whole economic system would come crashing down because it depends on trading commodities by risk-taking and the buying and selling of goods. The economy depends on urgency as a time-limitation to act now.

The God Beyond Organized Religion

will comfort me until the ghoulish apparition, the angel of mortality and a leviathan monster arrive to transport me to my next destination.[15]

I will die, as has been the protocol of mortality among living creatures for millenniums.[16] The demons for the deceased will carry the casket containing my body into its saintly season. I look back and see my body lying there, helpless in its depreciation. I remember the day I left my favorite car at the junkyard for scrap metal. I could imagine it calling out to me, pleading, "Please don't leave me here, I will run again, I promise." Isn't that weird? I couldn't look back. I felt so bad. It was just a car and it didn't make any sense to get new brakes with an odometer reading of 242 miles. What is really frightening is how easy it is to apply that same logic to a child living in an impoverished area. How can I just walk away? As I exit the door from her funeral/celebration, I am standing in the parking lot thinking, how can I just leave her there? How do parents leave their child behind in a funeral home? What will it be like to leave my body behind? Will I look back and regret not being able to take it with me?

I wonder what happens in those first few seconds of getting acclimated to my new normal. How will I know that I am actually dead and not just having a really strange sensation? Will I be aware that I have just died or will I think I am dreaming and asleep or daydreaming and awake? Will I try to pinch myself only to realize there is nothing to pinch? Do I open my eyes only to be met with darkness, my old friend, and then a laser summons me to follow with a sense of intrigue? Or will I dwell in the darkness, afraid, alone and helpless? Being alone would be the scariest part of death.[17] Death may be an altered state of consciousness. Will it feel like me but not me? I do not like the "not-knowing" what comes next. A bell

---

15. Is it like childbirth and we are in the womb, with our legs perched against the cervix, as the contractions try to spring us out?

16. Maybe there is nothing beyond this life. Does the function key of death delete us from existence? Is there a trash bin that holds our DNA for the time being until the divine operator deems it worthwhile to return to the inbox for reprocessing? What becomes of us when we are dumped in the trash bin? Does the god only think about us when we are in the inbox and forget about us when we are in draft mode? Are we sent elsewhere? Are we nothing more than an email message which communicates a thought and then once received, no longer has any usefulness? The possibility exists that we live this present life, have some good times, some bad, some struggles in-between and don't need to bother with self-enlightenment because instead of moving toward becoming more empathic persons we are only moving closer to death. When death comes to wipe us into oblivion, as long as we have had a good time, we are good to go.

17. I would also be afraid if I was unable to move my body.

The Purpose of Life, Death, and Dying

man will show me to my room and carry my bags and then ask, "Is there anything else I can do for you to make you feel comfortable?" I will respond kindly, "Yes please, provide an explanation of what is going on and by the way, where is everyone else?"

I would hope I would find other people there; at least one other person with whom to talk through what is happening as we wonder what is going on. I would prefer to be with someone I already knew but if among strangers, we could become friends by going through the experience together. My version of hell is a place of absolute isolation, where I cannot talk with others or share how I am feeling. Without the company of another human being, there would be no one who understands what I am feeling and no one for whom I can reflect what they may be feeling. I would like to think I could handle almost any situation if there is another person who can provide empathy for me and for whom I can empathize. Developing relationships here on earth may prepare us to connect with others when we die. It is the interaction between organic essences, the experience of intimacy which offers comfort when we are lonely or scared. Whatever happens when I die, I hope to god I am not alone.

Preferably, the people who serve on the heavenly hospitality committee will be people I have known here on earth and will be ecstatic to see me again (the moment of being reunited with all those who have gone before). Our deceased family members are likely the ones who do the meet and greet at the pearly gates. Oh, it will be so good to see my grandparents, aunts and uncles, a niece and nephew, a lifelong friend who also died of cancer in his early forties and every pet I ever had. The reunion will be bittersweet since I will have left all significant others back on earth (and I would never leave my children willingly). The committee will appear to me, clear as day, in some form I will recognize so I will not feel alone. I can handle anything as long as I am surrounded by people who have loved me and supported me and know how I am feeling and can anticipate what I need emotionally as I transition from life to death to the afterlife.

I will die and in seconds will open my eyes and look around and she will be there.[18] I see her coming towards me to give me a hug, just like we

---

18. Death is often described as an experience of "falling asleep" and yet, it is unclear whether one remains asleep until some guy blows a trumpet and all the bodies come out of the grave, dancing to the triumphant tune. In that case, at this moment she is not conscious and therefore not present but in some subdued state of semiconsciousness. I'm usually unconscious when I am asleep and being unconscious would not be coming back from the dead. I imagine that a few seconds or so after I die, I will awake and then know

The God Beyond Organized Religion

used to do when we met at the mall to go shopping or when we opened the door to greet each other. (We also used to give out an affectionate scream.) She smiles, and her expression lights up the heavenly sky; she is so happy to see me she is on cloud nine. I feel relieved she is there. After we embrace, she reassures me that death is nothing like it has been portrayed in the movies or in religious organizations. She will be in her glory to know more than me about the philosophy of religion (from her recent vantage point) and she will rise to the occasion bringing me up to speed with her newly acquired wisdom. Knowing me as well as she does, she will anticipate some of my immediate questions. "Can you eat anything you want and not gain weight?" and "Did you miss me?" and "Is there a god beyond organized religion?" Calmly and without missing a beat, she will answer my questions in the order asked, pulling back the great velvet curtain to reveal the secrets hidden from the view of the living.

In the first few minutes upon arrival, I would not want to be confronted with everything I did wrong here on earth.[19] I would not want to be ushered into a waiting room where one's anxiety goes sky high before making an appearance in the court of final judgment. The god of organized religion comes out from his chambers, looking very stern and serious and takes his chair while the rest of us stand in respect without reservation. It's the first time I have ever met him face to face so I am kind of in awe thinking, "OMG, this is the GMO!" Instead of giving me one of those big, ginormous hugs to make me feel good as he promised the whole time I was working for him on earth, he's not the warm fluffy I expected. He is frowning (not a good sign) as he reviews my record and I am standing before the

---

that there is an afterlife. I do not want to wait to wake up until some savior does some saving and the dead come dancing out of their graves, rejoicing in their newly acquired status of sainthood. It doesn't sound like they have to do anything meaningful to achieve this status (relying solely on the actions of the god).

19. If some guy has spent time making a laundry list of all my past indiscretions, lies and bad choices and thinks that this is the appropriate moment to recount each and every situation, I will not be a happy camper. Or worse, to update with modern technology, I have to sit through a video presentation, a synopsis of clips, one after another, showing me committing the act, a new way of confrontational judgment which cannot be refuted. Whereas in the old days, I suppose one could insist that it did not happen that way, today the judge points to the screen, conclusively identifying me as me and therefore responsible for the act. Does the judge really need to make a decision about whether I go to the wonderful place or whether I should be banished to hell? Does he take environmental (nurture) and epigenetic (nature) factors into account in his decision?

The Purpose of Life, Death, and Dying

bench feeling like a fool, like a school girl sent to the principal.[20] When I object, I am told to be quiet. When I ask for representation, I am told I have to represent myself. When I ask if I can be transferred to the court room of the god beyond organized religion, my request is denied.

He is shaking his head in disgust and I am thinking it would have been nice to die and be greeted by a god who said, "Well done and don't worry. None of those images of me they tout down there on earth is true." "Oh good," I breathe a sigh of relief. The god beyond organized religion will serve coffee and pastries and try to make me feel as comfortable as possible. As we reflect upon my experiences of life, this god will give me the benefit of the doubt that there were situations in which I thought I had made the right decision but later realized I might have chosen differently and would, if I could do it all over again. This god doesn't focus on what I did wrong; instead offers words of affirmation for the risks I took (which benefited others), the challenges I adapted to and the times I sacrificed my own needs for the greater good. I confess I feel bad about some of the things I did and this god simply says people make mistakes and if they can learn from them in the process of self-enlightenment then they are able to help others.

Back in the judgment room, the purpose of the review process is to ascertain who gets into heaven and who doesn't. A theology that weeds out some of the less desirable peons is perhaps the least convincing tenet of organized religion and stems from socioeconomic dynamics: we build ourselves up by making the afterlife an exclusive enterprise based on entrepreneurial drives. The thrill of the chase, the exhilaration of competition, the excitement of winning, impels this thinking. Yet, if we all come from the same place, it is likely we all go to the same place. If we believe everyone goes to heaven, then we may put a little more effort into learning how to get along with people who are culturally different from us. In heaven, we are no longer subdivided into cultural groupings. We might learn to treat each other with mutual respect if we could anticipate that these relationships will be critical to our contentment in the heavenly realm. Money, status and prestige will no longer matter.

I cannot imagine a gatekeeper-god who says to an adherent, "You belonged to a religious organization so you get to come in," or to the believer, "You believed in me so you get to come in," but to the agnostic or atheist, "You did not believe in me so you cannot come in." The god of organized

---

20. In my generation, one could be sent to the principal to kneel and check that one's skirt reached the floor.

religion seems to require people to be a member of a religious organization and he expects them to include a mention of the particular organization in their obituary (as well as in the eulogy). The adherent could do bad things during their lifetime but as long as they were sorry and attempted to make some amends, those bad things are forgiven. For the one who was not an adherent but a good person and always tried to do the right thing for other people, they may be granted a grace margin for two out of three. Belief and behavior (and the interplay between the two) seem to be the requirements for getting into heaven.

Organized religion has little to say about what we do in heaven or the purpose of going there for all eternity. They ask us to trust that the god has a reason and that that reason will be revealed after we die. If we do not know something, we are not meant to have access to that knowledge, which, like a five-year-old child, makes us imagine it worse than it really is. Heaven is a mystery that must be respected as such and any desire to speculate about what it must be like or what we do dishes the almighty. It's like a parent who doesn't tell their kids that they are going to Walt Disney World on vacation because they want them to be surprised once they get there. They might be just as surprised if told when the parent booked the trip and then they would have something to look forward to. I'm not sure I want to be surprised when I die and wake up on the blaster roller coaster headed straight down at a hundred miles an hour.

To compensate for this lack of information, organized religion focuses on two subjects: the décor of heaven and the requirements to get in. They concern themselves with curb appeal so that people will want to get in (or the requirements wouldn't really matter). Heaven is imaged with golden paved streets, puffy, fluffy clouds and pearly white gates. I am not sure why they think those images will appeal to people (I would have put the golf course on the brochure) but, whatever. Heaven is an exclusive country club and the management does their best to weed out the riffraff. Their reputation rests on being exclusive that some get in and others don't because if everybody got it then no one would want to go there (?). The undesirables might ruin heaven's reputation. If you make anything something that everyone wants, then no matter what actually is, everyone is "dying" to get in.

Whether she got into heaven or hell is not a relevant question for me. St. Peter might say to her, "Well done, my faithful servant, you have deserved entrance into the kingdom of heaven; but there are those who did not fare as well as you, who did what they needed to do to survive and feed

The Purpose of Life, Death, and Dying

their children, but they stole and so they are destined for hell." She would not join a private club which was exclusive toward any group of people. If she knew that hell was a horrible place, she would advocate for those who were denied admission, come to their defense, use her lawyer skills to exonerate those who were being cast into confinement. She would demand, "Until you free everyone from hell, I'm not going to heaven." She would gather others to occupy purgatory and protest until those who were in hell were released. In her thinking, those who go straight to heaven without defending the helpless, the marginalized and the oppressed and only list their own accomplishments on the application don't deserve to go to a better place than others.

I am also fairly certain she wouldn't go anywhere that isn't pet friendly. Over the years, she had a number of dogs, Ally, Luke, Joel and Abel; the last three were rescued greyhounds. She cared fervently about animal rights. We would go to the mall and visit every cosmetic counter and ask if the makeup they were selling had been tested on animals. She posted pictures of dogs that had been abused at the hands of those who participated in the heinous act of dog fighting. She struggled to feel any compassion toward those who pitted two dogs against each other for entertainment (gambling). She used to say unless we understand why the perpetrators do this, what makes them so traumatized that they have lost the ability to have empathy toward dogs (much less human beings), we will not be able to know how to prevent and stop dog fighting.[21] She never ceased in her efforts to educate the public about its prevalence, profiling areas where it was likely to occur and lobbying politicians to change the laws. Her passion for the dogs came from a place deep within her own soul that harbored a feeling of helplessness.

That helplessness pervades our being through much of our lifetime. Hovering over the face of the earth waiting for one of those creatures to be vulnerable, is a mischievous sprite named Lilith, who claims her next victim, often with no warning that she is coming. I was walking around Baltimore inner harbor yesterday with a friend and I thought to myself, I could get a call tomorrow that something has happened to her. If one friend can die, then another friend can die. No one is safe from Lilith. Her lingering omnipresence, opaque in appearance and a forgery in form, awaits a precious moment to transition a breathing being from ordinary existence to otherworldly "nonexistence." She does not adhere to rules of justice or

---

21. Yes, I believe she would still want the perpetrators of violence to go to heaven.

The God Beyond Organized Religion

fairness as some are in the prime of their life, in excellent physical shape and hold so much promise and potential to contribute to making an impact upon this universe while others beg for her visit waiting patiently by the window for any glimpse of her.

No living being is exempt from this possibility. All the money, power, prestige cannot purchase a pass. Her inevitability is the one certainty of life. We have little idea of what will happen tomorrow or what our life might be like ten years from now but we do know that at a time in the future, somewhere down the road, life we will cease to be. No more ice cream Sundaes, movies on Friday nights, dinners out with friends, barbecues with family, and so on. In a hundred years, no one will even remember who I am or what I did upon this earth. My great, great grandchildren will have to ask their parents my name to fill in a genogram for their school project. I will not only cease to exist, memory of me will be erased from the universe's collective consciousness. Traces of me may continue to be decipherable in DNA, but no one will be able to recall a good story about me. Not only will my physical presence be obsolete, my signature will be insignificant and my contribution to this world will long be forgotten.

I guess I am still stuck on the finality of death. Its inevitability makes me feel helpless. I am never going to see her again (upon earth) and I just can't seem to get past that. We are never going to go to her beach house again and walk along the shore. We are never going to go out to dinner as couple friends, getting all dressed up and enjoying each other's company. With our husbands, we once ate dinner in New York City at the Tavern on the Green and after midnight, took a carriage ride around Central Park. When the horse rider asked where she wanted to go, she wanted to see the apartment where John Lennon had lived and died. It was freezing and we were all under a blanket as the driver pointed this place out to us. We are never going to do such cool things again. We are never going to drink watermelon wine coolers and talk philosophy and theology.

CHAPTER 8

The Recycling of One's Organic Essence
The Afterlife

The last time we spent together we went to her beach house and stayed up till 2:30 in the morning, retelling all the stories we have retold a thousand times. We hadn't done this for years and looking back now, I pause and ponder, how eerie that we would engage in a session of "remember the time" when she was so close to dying. To do so, transported us back in time when we could relive the experience all over again. Just now, as I write this, I feel as if I am back there. I can see her sitting on the sofa, laughing and tossing back her long curly hair, the smell of the sea salt in the air, the humid heat of a summer night, sipping a watermelon wine cooler and laughing some more. When I close my eyes, I can see her so vividly, it's just so hard to grasp she is no longer here. Had I known that this was going to be our last time together, I wouldn't have wanted to do anything different. I'm sure she would have told me if she knew and I would have begged her not to go. If she had known, we would have arranged a sign so that she could let me know when she arrived in heaven, she was OK.

As I write this, I am in a room with a large picture window overlooking the front of the house. Long branches of a big tree swing across the window and a bird comes and sits on one of those branches, looking right at me. The bird's movement captures my attention and I look up for a moment to make eye contact. When our eyes meet, the bird tilts its head in a knowing pose, just slight to be recognizable. Initially, the interaction makes me feel kind of strange because I am looking at a bird and a bird is looking at me.

And yet, there is something familiar about it that cannot be put into words, an intriguing something which makes me curious and suspicious. Just at the moment I wonder if it is her, reappearing in the form of a bird to let me know that her soul is still among the living, it flutters away with the wings soaring above the clouds. The plausibility of creaturely incarnation doesn't seem farfetched when one is not afraid to think outside the bird cage.

In a strange and peculiar sort of way, I can feel her presence with me. It neither provides comfort nor produces distress. Just an intuitive feeling, an eccentric experience which you realize almost immediately *is out of the ordinary*. Even though I can't see her or hear her voice, I sense she tries to communicate with me in whatever ways she can. Whenever there is a significant moment in writing this book, she shuffles my iPod and likes to play her favorite songs. I don't know that I would have ever written this book had it not been for these signs of encouragement. There have also been moments when I think she is writing the book and I am just moving my fingers on the keyboard. I don't mean to sound out there or weird in my thinking about this, only to entertain some ideas that are not within the scope of conventional wisdom as supplied by organized religion.

I wonder if she knows what is happening down here on earth. Is there a skylight on this planet that those in heaven can see through to see? If she can make contact with me, can she see what I am doing? Does she know how difficult it has been for me to lose my best friend? Can one have empathy from heaven? If she can see me, is she watching when I am pooping or having sex? Yikes, that's disturbing. Does she know that I am writing a book about her and our experiences together to make sense of god? Does she know the book is written in her memory? Is she reading over my shoulder what I am writing and at times, slapping my shoulder and saying, "Don't write that!" or, "No one is going to get that, write it a different way," or, "I'm not sure I understand the middle section." Through most of the writing, she has been smiling and whispering words of encouragement and support and filling me with ideas I would not have thought of on my own.

I wonder if those who love us and die and go to heaven can advocate for us or intercede on our behalf to make good things happen to us in our best interests. Maybe when the forces of bad threaten to align themselves in formation to bring about devastation, she can intervene to rearrange. Maybe when the god wants to bring about punishment or continue with the master plan, she can ask to change the course of things. Maybe when some huge happening is about to befall humanity, she can argue, "Don't do it," and the god will refrain from implementation. She knew my fears, wishes, hopes and dreams. I would trust her to make decisions for me. I try to be aware of moments when I am afraid and wonder if she can do something to alleviate the threat. I know that, if she could, she would. I believe all this is plausible as it is transformative and not transactional. If she does help me when I need help, there is nothing I can do for her.

She would know I would be wondering about the matters of life and death and the afterlife. She now has access to the answers we spent our lifetimes trying to figure out. She is now privy to this knowledge, the secrets revealed, data gathered. She now knows. Whatever did not make sense to us when she was among the living now makes sense to her. She now knows what happens after death and I am sure she is eager to share all this with me. It must be killing her not to be able to just call me up and tell me. Or, she is trying to leak information. I can imagine there are things she is trying to tell me that I just don't get. I need to remain receptive to new ideas and thoughts about the afterlife and let her expertise shine through in some of those dark places. I need to work at managing my anxiety (about my own death) so that I will be able to imagine her experience of the afterlife.

I envision she has plopped herself down in front of some large screen television that records the daily show. She surfs the channels checking in on family and friends and pets to see what they are doing and how they are getting along without her. When someone she knows pops up on the screen, she feels overwhelmed with sadness. She wishes she could go back. She doesn't obsess about this desire because she knows that creatures can't go back, at least in their original form. She regrets that she did not get the chance to live out her life and feels resentful that she died so young. Life doesn't always work out the way we expect. She still wants to be my best friend but she considers whether or not that will prevent me from going out and finding a new one with whom to laugh and share life's experiences and she doesn't want to get in the way of that pursuit. It's hard for her when she sees me trying to fill that void but she knows there will always be a special place in my heart where she resides.

I hope she has better things to do in heaven than sitting around all day concerned over the happenings on earth. I wonder what she does all day long. Does heaven get internet or cable service? Some fear being alone. Some fear not being able to move one's body, others fear intense pain. I fear boredom. I am deathly afraid of not having anything to do (even if tedious and meaningless). I also don't want someone to think of something for me to do just to give me something to do. If I get to heaven and someone hands me a pair of wings and says, "Wear the uniform," and directs me to sing with the heavenly host sitting on a puffy cloud strumming harps of god, I will request a transfer. My version of hell would be having nothing to do all day long or being able to think of things that I could be doing but not be able to do. I would think providing entertainment must be a major challenge for the heavenly staff. Without something to do (and everyone likes to do different things), eternity would seem like an awful long time.

I envision heaven is like a high-end resort with all the amenities to play which the rich never had time to do and the rest of us never had the money to do. Heaven is camp for the deceased. Complete with swimming pools, golf courses and beautiful beaches stretching as far as the eye can see, and snow skiing (heaven has climate control) are just some of its picturesque surroundings. I will get to walk my dogs (yes, you get to have pets in heaven) along the seashore. For the less active, one can go to the spa and get a massage, beauty treatment or lounge by the beach reading a book. An attendant serves drinks with colorful umbrellas, filled with calories but that doesn't matter because we have no body per se. A few donuts for breakfast, followed by an ice cream sundae for lunch and a box of chocolates for dinner and we are good to go. Everything pleasurable on earth we will be available to do in heaven (especially those things that we never seemed to find the time to do or couldn't afford).

I imagine that heaven is like a vacation from life. We die and go to heaven for an overhaul, a reboot, a tune-up, time apart from the routine of earthly existence. We hang around all day in hammocks, leisurely enjoying the sun and the sand. Everyone experiences the same things, e.g., good food, perfect surroundings, great views. Nothing costs so no one needs any money. Most people are cordial to each other and if there are no lounge chairs left on the deck will jump up and say, "here, take mine, I need to go get something to eat." We've had an entire lifetime to worry about money, children, relationships, body image, the planet, hunger and equality; it's nice to take a break from our problems. Up here, we don't concern ourselves with earthly issues, unless of course that whole global warming thing continues to get so out of control that it begins polluting our beautiful, plush heavenly abode. We all wear T-shirts that say, "Afterlife is good" (in different colors). Heaven is a nice place to visit but I wouldn't want to live there forever.

The Recycling of One's Organic Essence

What I don't want to hear are those words that the god of organized religion has had his arm twisted to tout: "She's in a better place." No place could be better than trying on shoes at the Natick Collection Mall on a Saturday afternoon. No place could be better than "her beach" where we would stroll for hours and hours, letting the cuff of our capris touch the ever-receding surf and feeling the sand massage the soul of our feet, as we talked and laughed and cried and laughed and talked. There could be no better place than sitting on bar stools in an upscale, chic, contemporary restaurant, sipping drinks in the style of the stars, feeling glamorous, confident and emotionally connected. I cannot imagine any place she would think was better than being with her family, friends and dogs, even if it entailed living in deplorable conditions. What made everything better was that she had relationships with people and pets who loved and cared about her.

In fairness to the better place theology, let us play this out with magical/wishful thinking. Consider a cafeteria where all carbohydrates are created equal and we can eat anything we want and not gain weight. Not bad. I would like that. Or, a place where we don't have to do housework, like laundry, vacuuming,[1] mowing the grass, cleaning the toilet, etc., would be a welcome relief.[2] A place where you don't argue with your partner, it is sunny every day and everyone treats each other the way that they would want to be treated. In a better place, everyone would freely exercise congeniality. A place where I felt I had a reason to be there, a sense of purpose and meaning and the skills needed (or I could learn) to fulfill that mission would be really, really attractive. But better than being with my present friends and family? I think not.

The "better place" theology suffers from a major methodological flaw regarding socioeconomics: what constitutes "better" may not be shared from a universal perspective. What it means to be poor depends on how a society determines a baseline for "enough" resources to sustain the body and mind's health. One group may consider owning a vacuum cleaner and indoor toilet as luxury items (presuming you own a rug that needs vacuuming and have access to a place to poop connected to a water pipeline). A better place, in the mind of those who are refugees moving away from political oppression, may be the freedom to set up a tent and not worry about

---

1. If I get to heaven and the god puts me in charge of vacuuming and tells me to make the vacuum sing, I will not think it a better place.

2. Although when I feel something is happening to me helpless, one thing I can control is cleaning the house. Cleaning can actually make me feel better.

The God Beyond Organized Religion

a bunch of rebels coming into the community to pillage the resources one has managed to carry thus far in a blanket on their back. Only the middle class look forward to changing locations to move up to purchase a bigger house can imagineer a "better place."

The better place rose theology is fraught with thorny thinking.[3] It assumes that we would be happier in different surroundings, a hook which drives the accumulation of wealth. In our present social location, we are consumed by uncomfortable feelings, and so we envisage that if we move to a different place, those feelings will be left behind. If only we could buy a house on the Florida coast, then we will be happy. Our relationship with our spouse will suddenly return to the romantic phase and we will fall in love all over again. If only we could get away on a cruise for a couple of weeks, all our problems would dissolve into pretty alcoholic drinks with cute little colorful umbrellas. If only we could exchange our current circumstances for a better home, with a better wife and better children and if we were better at our job so that we would get a promotion, then finally, we would be happy. Like a drippy chocolate chip ice cream cone held at a distance, we respond by making a slight adjustment[4] which we presume will put it all within reach.

Religious people tend to repeat these non-scriptural phrases so they do not have to think for themselves and say something that might actually be a source of strength to another in their moment of weakness.[5] Conventional clichés are a dime a dozen, and religious writings replete with pithy petite phrases that can easily be taken out of context and reshuffled for a custom fit to the current condition. I do not want some religious person to come along and say, "She is in a better place." I don't want to hear, "God must have a good reason for taking her away from us," or that "God must need her more than we do," because this world is in worse shape without her. These sayings are a way to create emotional distance between the one who is repeating them from the one who is grieving. Instead of developing empathy by imagining what it must be like to lose your best friend to

---

3. My best definition of "thorny thinking" is thinking that looks good initially and then in time makes one feel bad. Thorns hurt and make people bleed.

4. An example would be the wife who divorces her husband of twenty years because she wants to find herself.

5. All they need to do is to imagine someone saying these statements to them and they would realize that they are not helpful and hopefully wouldn't say them any longer. "God must need her more than you do." "This is part of God's great plan, even if we don't understand it." OMG! Really? If someone said those things to you, would you feel better?

The Recycling of One's Organic Essence

cancer, these phrases are used as the default position in lieu of doing the adaptive work.

Many times we anticipate that an experience will bring us greater joy than it actually does. We plan a vacation and then when we get there, our problems seem to stow away in our luggage. We put a lot of hope into the planning and dreaming and this helps us to get through some of our more complicated hardships. We talk about going to our "happy place" where life is simpler (and we can get there by closing our eyes and imagining a surrounding which brings us a sense of inner-peace). What tends to happen, however, is that after we unpack and settle into our new digs, we get to the beach and lie down on our lounge chair and think to ourselves, "Now what am I going to do?" While we have entertained a fantasy about how good this is going to be to "get away," now we are trying to figure out what that means in practice. If I get there and get bored, I will realize I have arrived at hell, not heaven.

Eventually our ultra-ultimate spiritual retreat at the heavenly spa will get old. The day will come when we are lying in our hammock, looking out over the ocean and become aware we are ready to do something else. Our organic essence will tug on our hearts and persuade us we need to engage in meaningful activities to help ourselves or others or we are taking up space, breathing precious air. If there isn't a purpose for our existence, why should the god beyond continue to pay for the services of the heavenly staff? If we don't find ourselves in a situation to find the energy to be empathic toward others, what does god have to do with any of this? It is possible that the god needs a break as well and is hanging in the next hammock. As nice as all this sounds for those of us whose current life involves emotional pain and intense suffering, if this is all I have to do for eternity, I would be better off being snuffed out of existence.

There would have to be a real good reason for keeping our organic essence eternal or at least expanding its shelf life. Recycling souls is environmentally friendly (reducing the carbon emissions at the baby-making plant). Is it cost effective not to create new babies? Is it environmentally constructive to recycle the organic essence of those in heaven? Is the god beyond organized religion modeling for us the reasons why we should be recycling here on earth? Why not just make everything anew? Is the idea of something more than this present lifetime, nothing more than wishful thinking, especially for those who have had such a tough life? Does the imagery of heaven help us remain hopeful that our present suffering (especially as a preface to death) has a happy ending? Or does the organic essence accumulate internal knowledge that makes it better adapted to be empathic toward the suffering of others in the next life? Perhaps the experiences in our past lives are what help us to achieve self-enlightenment.

If it is plausible that we go to heaven to recharge the battery of our organic essence, then it is likely that we do not stay there long. When we are ready to go back to earth and live another life, we say to the god beyond, "OK. Send me back. I'm ready to return." Just as we get to choose when we want to let go of life (with the exception of an accidental death), we get to choose when we want to retrieve it. It's a hard decision to make because we don't get to return as the person we were in our former life. Our organic essence enters a new body and will develop a new occupational extract. I don't think we have to return as the same species of creature and perhaps get to choose from the vast array of creatures that crawl, swim and walk upon the earth. (I think I was a cat in a former life and got hit by a car.) Because I can still feel her with me, I would guess that her organic essence is still in heaven. I know there will come a day when she will make this decision and return to earth in the body of another and I will accept when this day comes.

My occupational extract has served me well. It has been my thinking mechanism to sort through, express and transform my emotions arising from life's experiences. It helped me to make sense of these experiences in such a way that changed the way I was feeling, e.g., from helpless to empowered to help myself and others. My occupational extract reflected on why I do the things I do and helped me to make sense of why I think that things are the way they are and what I can do to transform them (as well as accept the things I cannot change). But I will not need it after I die. In heaven, the occupational extract is emptied of its current storage, returned to manufacturer settings so that its technology can live on in another, yet-to-be-born individual. The contents of the occupational extract live on in our descendants: our children, grandchildren, great nieces and nephews and all those who loved us. The transfer takes place during our lifetime. You cannot take your occupational extract with you when you die. You wouldn't want to because it is filled with the aftereffects of trauma and it is tired.

My organic essence has also served me well. It too has been the recipient of important data on its thumb drive preserved in eternal storage. Our memories of times past, thoughts and feelings that we didn't tell to anyone (you can take some things to your grave), the sacred center of your mission

The Recycling of One's Organic Essence

control, the hard drive which allowed or denied access to all software applications, all represent who we are inside.[6] The organic essence goes to heaven for recharging and stays there for quite a preset period of time (not for eternity) so as to sort through some of the things that happened on earth. Heaven is a battery recharging station that empties me of everything that has ever weighed heavy on my heart and allows me to push replay and see situations in my lifetime that bring me either comfort or challenge so that I can learn to let go and let it be.[7] My experience in heaven is a sabbatical from earthly existence granting me time to appreciate the things that I did on earth and preparing me to return to do meaningful things once again that contribute to the common good.

When we return to the earth with our organic essence, there is some data retained on that hard drive. We form a new occupational extract which interprets the data, but the essential "me" lives on forever and ever. This is why we feel we have had some experiences before because traces of our memory can be recalled through spiritual practices. We may visit a certain place and feel as if we have been there before. We may meet someone for the first time who we swear we have met in the past. I wonder if we return to earth in the same family in which we have always been. For instance, a baby born into the family may be the recycled essence of a great grandparent. I don't know how this works, yet maybe we come back to earth to find our soul mate who is the same person we were married to in our former life. This may prompt us to be kinder, gentler and more compassionate toward those who come after us and those with whom we share our present lives. Even though families can be complicated relationships and thrive on dysfunctional dynamics, they are the source of forming an occupational extract.

If there is life after death, as the great oak testifies when her leaves wither to the ground in autumn only to be reborn in the spring, heaven (or the whereabouts of the afterlife) will offer a different experience than here on earth.[8] To merely replicate our experiences on earth brings with it

---

6. If we were a computer, our organic essence is the hard drive and our occupational extract is the software.

7. Perhaps heaven is a reflective retreat center offering counseling so that we can let go of our regrets, disappointments and frustrations to move forward to begin again.

8. One of the most compelling reasons for life after death and a god who is the drawbridge in-between is because there are so many people who hold onto the hope that their suffering will eventually cease. Only the middle and upper class can entertain atheism because they don't think they need anything from the god beyond organized religion. If

The God Beyond Organized Religion

all the potential problems, heartache and hardships. Even though heaven has no qualitative difference than earth, they both have their positives and negatives each experience contributes to the functionality of our organic essence. I have depicted heaven as being surrounded by luxury, a nice place to be filled with high octane energy to feel good but if you have spent your life being catered to you will be disappointed when no pool boys show up to bring you a drink when you put up your flag. If I have spent my life food insecure in a politically charged and oppressive climate, heaven is a wonderful place because there are no checkpoints (and I have freedom of movement).

I suppose heaven could be a happy place owned by the workers. Perhaps the creator god graciously bowed out of the design phase for this location and empowered the creatures to determine their own destiny and create their own version of heaven. Maybe heaven has nothing to do with a super-power conglomerate and does not function like some big corporation in the sky. Family owned or a small business, it has that personal touch and offers good service and good food. The god beyond doesn't need to super-control what happens there and trusts that when the creatures have what they need and appreciate that this is so, treat each other with respect and dignity. If the heavenly staff micromanages this behavior by setting forth rules, posted on the pearly gates, people will behave differently towards each other than if they do so because they believe in a god beyond organized religion. Then each person will exercise compassion and understanding toward others *and* expect nothing in return.

---

the god can't do anything for them to improve their station in life, then the god doesn't exist in anyone else's life either.

CHAPTER 9

Reflections on the Search
The Whereabouts Question Revisited: Where Do We Go to Encounter God?

The Epistemological Question: How Do We Know?

The Ontological Question: Does the God Beyond Exist?

When we were children, my father dragged us up most of the mountains in New Hampshire's presidential range.[1] He would be a hundred yards ahead of us, moving at a steady pace, while we lagged behind, complaining our legs hurt and whining we wanted to turn around (and run as fast as we could downhill until we fell and rolled). To encourage us to continue moving upward, even though that direction is more challenging and involves the exertion of greater energy, he would promise the reward of a candy bar (and reaching the summit was but the objective to that goal). Every time we rose above the alpine zone and took in the breathtaking views of the other mountains and the lakes and the clouds hovering just above our heads, we would stand in awe and reverence before the tremendous mystery. Reaching in our backpacks for our Kodak cameras to capture the moment on film, we learned that a change in our

---

1. As adults he no longer had to drag us. Now we have the honor of dragging our own children.

The God Beyond Organized Religion

view of the world also changes the way in which we connect within it. My father knew where to encounter the god beyond organized religion.

Hiking is a spiritual practice. The very act of physically moving makes people feel spiritual and thus receptive to an experience transcending transcendence. Movement makes one willing to keep going even when one doesn't feel like it or want to. Given that we live in a culture of convenience, people do not willingly exert energy unless they anticipate a benefit. No one can promise an encounter with god and one might have to exercise one's spiritual muscles for quite some time before one feels it (whatever "it" may be). Movement allows one to let go of what one has always believed about god; to reexamine one's concept in light of an experience to promote meaning-making. Those of you who have joined me thus far have likely made some connections between your own experiences and concept of god. This is a very different approach than religious organizations would have us do. I am not all that interested in finding the god beyond organized religion as I am to inspire the reader to move beyond the conventional, systematic method of doing theology.[2]

The path we have treaded has zigzagged, curved and meandered. Moving from the dark side of the moon into a bright light of insight offers two paths from which to choose (and there is still time to change the path you are on). While both paths begin at sea level and therefore require the same amount of energy to the summit, one path appears to be less of an incline but may unexpectedly have a sudden unexplained decline.[3] The other path has a slow, gradual incline with rocks positioned as footstools for ease of movement but which demands the skill set of immediate decision-making. It is not the quickest way to the top which makes meaning from an

---

2. My theological wanderings have led me above the tree line, the alpine zone, the balcony of branches, the sky view; any metaphoric mindset that means "to see above earthly undertones." All I am doing is thinking about things that people don't often take the time to think about or going to a different place in order to get a different perspective. I have attempted to cross over to an otherworldly orientation to see things differently. I realize that there were probably times when I sounded incoherent, and the reader likely saw some inconsistencies that tugged to be teased. In one room I was the academic and in another, the grieving friend writing as if in a bubbling blog/bog. I feel no compulsion to have to choose one word as preferable to another, nor to make them compete for status as being the right word. The reader may have deciphered literary codes revealing more about my journey than the written word itself. Process can help us gain insight into content.

3. The risk here is that sometimes decline can get one into a valley in which one has to find one's way.

experience. Confronting challenges and observing obstacles can shift one's perspective and will equip one with new and improved coping skills for future crises. Plowing ahead at full speed to "make it work" and "get over it" may not be the most productive path even if it gets one to where everyone else is going. Constantly moving without time for self and other-reflection is the surest way to go through life void of purpose and significance.

Cave living has become normative in our society. Religion is practiced as a sedentary, private and individual undertaking. I don't know those who live in the cave next to me and I don't make much effort to get to know them. If they can't do anything for me, I have no reason to invest energy into forming relationships. The reason why people do not give a portion of their income to help the poor is, "What have they ever done for me?" or, "What would they be able to do for me when I need help?" Without a security bond printed from the bank of reciprocity, the code of transactional relationships, it becomes difficult to get people to care about people who live next door (never mind in faraway lands). When asked why they do not recycle, repurpose or reuse, some will respond, "What do I care? I won't be around in fifty years." Getting people to care about others is the adaptive challenge we face when we seek to solve social problems. I have argued that developing empathy is quintessential to this process.

Before this experience, I was a cave dweller myself; the loss of my best friend motivated me to get out of the comfort of my surroundings and re-evaluate my life in relation to others and to the god.[4] While I have made something good come out of something bad (becoming more empathic), I am not glad this has happened to me. Her death has been one of the most devastating experiences of my life. I have begun to move forward because I know I cannot go back. I have visited places within me that I did not know existed and in my suffering, connected with the suffering of others. I care

---

4. Losing my best friend to cancer has inspired me to reexamine my concept of god. I suppose I believe in the god of organized religion, having been raised in a culture obligated to do so. I kind of thought everyone should believe in god for the sake of society. I no longer feel that way. I don't believe in some old guy waiting for me to do something wrong to do me in. I cannot imagine a god with extreme power who requires me to help others if I want to get into heaven. It doesn't make any sense to me to believe in a god who seeks to sustain an unequal distribution of needed resources and human rights. The god of organized religion is holding me back, keeping me from moving forward toward self-enlightenment. I just don't seem to be able to go where I want to go with the god of organized religion. I can no longer believe in a god who trades right belief and good behavior for divine favors. For when I needed this god to do his divine dealings, when I needed him to save her from death, he did nothing.

The God Beyond Organized Religion

about others and want to do all that I can to address the social problems of poverty, equality and global warming. By letting go of a transactional god, I have changed the way I relate to family and friends. I can do nice things for others, show loving-kindness in my interactions and engage in acts of compassion. I need nothing in return because I believe in a god who needs nothing in return.

Before religion became organized, people experienced being religious through physical movement such as dance or pilgrimage to sacred sites.[5] Moving the body in rhythm to the beat of an instrument helped people to feel spiritually connected to the gods. Organic religion (pre-organized) made no distinction between "being religious" and "being spiritual" (or "being" anything for that matter) and thus spirituality/religiosity was part of every aspect of everyday life. Religion takes root when founders receive a transformative message from the god with whom they had experienced a recent encounter. Adherents, in their excitement and enthusiasm to have a similar encounter, spread the message to foreign lands to convert new believers.[6] Religion was on the move because it helped people to handle hardships and make sense of them within their cultural environment.

Organic religion did not distinguish between "religion" and "culture" or anything else for that matter and believed that the gods had something to do with the forces of nature and their unpredictability (pre-Weather Channel). The gods controlled the rain and the sun and the thunder and the floods. Acts of god often mirrored the social drama of the divine tier.[7] Lightening was an expression of one god's anger toward another god for flirting with its spouse and the earth was the stage upon which the performance was enacted. The gods had mood swings reflected in their mood rings. Organic religion functioned to appease the gods so that they would work through nature to help people meet their basic needs.[8] The produce

---

5. What I didn't want to do was to stay put. I had this intense need to move. I am one of those people who move about all the time. I don't like to sit still; it makes me feel like I am not being productive. If I sit still, I am afraid I will get depressed. So I pack my day with things to do to remain busy and the more stuff I can check off my list at the end of the day, the better I feel about myself.

6. The new believers could then tweak the religious practices to be relevant to their own cultural environment.

7. Assigning natural phenomena to god's actions is one of the last vestiges of organized religion and has only recently been deleted from insurance policies for property damage.

8. Here I am essentially answering the question, "Can the god beyond morph into different functions as the needs of society change?"

Reflections on the Search

of a bountiful harvest was all the proof that anyone needed that the gods were active in the world.[9]

Before religion became organized, whole cultures grew religion on the very ground where the god made its residence. With roots firmly planted by ancestral anthologies, the gods had power over a particular plot of land. Those displaced to another land as a consequence of war or famine shifted their allegiance to the god of this new land (gods were immovable across national borders and thus confined to a particular area). Which god to whom one should express devotion was determined by where one lived and worked and farmed and danced. This god squeezed the clouds to sprinkle the rain upon the seed and made the sprouts yield an abundance of fruits and vegetables. In time, beliefs changed and large clans began migrating and bringing their own gods with them and religion took on new forms/expressions as it became integrated with incoming cultures. This allowed for residents to be tolerant of diverse religious views (the worship of multiple gods on the same land), a tolerance that we struggle with today.

Once religion took root on rocky ground, its survival depended on being organized. Religious organizers organized people to form a religious organization. Religion became branded as "religion:" a set of rituals and practices contained in a building and formatted with rules and bylaws and employed with hierarchical staff, from a senior-something to a youth group leader.[10] Their job is to wave a carrot, enticing god to want to come inside to be present to the adherents. When nothing seems to tantalize him to take up transient residence, they are reminded of him with transitional objects such as symbols, idols and icons. While they patiently pause, they are not dancing and having fun in the pursuit of religious fervor as their ancestors experienced god, now they sit passively on unpadded seats, listening to leaders ask for supplication (and money), invoking his presence through prayer and other tangential tactics of transcendence.[11] Meanwhile, adherents hope that god will notice the carrot and respond accordingly.

Organized religion presumes that god comes to the people; organic religion believes that people should actively pursue an encounter with the god. Therefore, to go in search for the god beyond organized religion, we have been physically moving through natural surroundings, places where

---

9. Creation gods can act independently in the world and don't need creatures. The gods of organic religion were almost all involved in acts of creation.

10. I forgot to mention that judicatory officials oversee denominational polity.

11. Passivity is the position of preference.

The God Beyond Organized Religion

organic religion was grown, where people experienced the immanence of the gods.[12] As we converse about and traverse through philosophical crossings into the strange wilderness of theology, we have not been sitting in beach chairs, drinking watermelon wine coolers by the seashore. A sedentary stance of meditative musings did not produce the desired result of finding the god beyond organized religion. My hypothesis is that this god can be encountered through physical and emotional movement: moving the body (and if one is unable to do this, imagining moving the body) so as to move the mind in new directions.[13]

I don't know if the god beyond organized religion exists. I have no way of knowing the answer to that question with conviction or certainty. Those who believe in the god of organized religion do not claim to know the answer either, for they depend on faith as the belief in things that cannot (and perhaps should not) be subject to scientific proof.[14] If axial measurements of statistics could be calculated to prove beyond reasonable doubt, faith would no longer be considered an acceptable substitute. If it were possible to substantiate that there is some kind of a god who has some power to act in the universe, either independently as organized religion professes or through the creatures as I have proposed, our society would no longer need to provide opportunities for a conversion experience. If tomorrow night the god beyond organized religion made an appearance on Larry King and

---

12. If someone has a disability preventing them from physical movement, another person should carry them and the person being carried should contribute to the conversation by describing their own point of view.

13. To keep everyone entertained while they wait for the god, organized religion does put on a show or mass or service. Leaders talk and everyone else has to be silent. My father's generation listened to the radio and then could go to a religious organization and listen to a twenty minute sermon/teaching, but my generation didn't develop those auditory skills. After a few minutes, I am pushing buttons trying to figure out how to change the picture screen. I want to interact with what I hear and see to encounter the god. Listening to how someone else found god bores me to tears.

14. On this path, we do not need to dichotomize theology from science because philosophy likes both. She is the friend who unites them. Science too works for people who want her to find certain things that will confirm their interests. When there is tension between theology and science, between theories of how the universe came into being and the origin of the human species, philosophy may serve as a good mediator. Philosophy doesn't work for anybody. She's been unemployed because she refuses to serve the interests of organizations and their hierarchical needs. Infrequently she is offered as a course in the humanities department but most students of life shy away from her because she sounds high maintenance. Anyway, she likes science and theology and both can trust her. She wants people to think things out and she helps them to do just that.

Reflections on the Search

was convincing enough, we would abandon the search. Proof would be the demise of organized religion, not its savior.

Science seems to have emerged as a threat to religion as if she stuck a pin in the balloon of belief. Organized religion is so easily offended by the interests of science, and yet, science did not set out to disprove (or prove) the existence of a god. Science could care less about religion; it's only since science has some social status that religion thinks it is trying to dethrone its platform and dismiss its portfolio. Science seeks to advance science, the knowledge of the workings of the world; its method of inquiry rivaling the fact that results can be replicated (and not attributed to the mood swings of the gods). Science is not concerned with whether or not a god exists. To suggest that science has any investment in religious workings or wanderings or wish-fulfilling fantasies would risk its ethical mandate not to practice outside its field of expertise. Science is smarter than that.

When we began this journey together, I stated that I had no intention of walking the ontological path. I have changed my mind (which I might do again before this manuscript goes to the publisher). I continue to have no interest in convincing the reader of my position. Instead, I have sought to expose the interests of socioeconomics in promoting one concept of god over another. Having expended much effort to examine the options of this alternative construct, I thought it would at least be fun to entertain the possibility (rather than weigh the probability) that such a god exists and if there is any observable evidence. However, we shall only wander around in the "what-if" woods; that is, what if a god beyond organized religion does exist? If such a god exists, would it make a difference in how a society approaches contemporary social problems? Would it make a difference if everyone believed that this god exists?

What do we mean by "exist'? The word "existence" implies a changing being; that which comes into (temporal) existence and can just as easily move into the realm of "nonexistence." If god is eternal, everlasting, has always been, is now and shall always be, this may imply we cannot talk about "existence" as if there is no possibility for "nonexistence." If we engage in a semantic study for what we call "objects" that are said to be "permanent," then we may get closer to what we mean, but then, we risk objectifying the divine to having no personality factors we associate with being a creature, such as feeling, creative impulses and the capacity for love. The god beyond may be timeless or rather not bound to the construct we have concluded to be "time." God is in the empathy for others. Because creatures have been

The God Beyond Organized Religion

empathic since the dawn of creaturely-design, we may conclude that the god beyond has always been in existence.

If there is a god, either one who works for organized religion or one residing within the creatures, neither has done a particularly good job of making itself known.[15] Even though I can see god in the beauty of a forest and in the tranquility of a river, I cannot see god in the animal rescue shelter or the poverty-stricken neighborhood just streets from my house. Even though I can see god in a rally for the right to marry, I cannot see god in the waiting room when a partner is denied access to the intensive care unit. Even though I can see god waiting in the line to recycle electronics that might have ended up in a landfill, god seems to be among the missing in environments where fracking is done by powerful fuel companies. Organized religion asks its adherents to trust that god is working behind the scenes "to make everything better" even though we can only see him working in some places and not in others. It doesn't seem to occur to them that god might need us to be the ones to improve our living conditions for everyone on this earth.

The god of organized religion doesn't want to be seen (especially his face) but has an intense and immense desire to be known. He wants people to come into a religious organization and then brag to others about how they ran into him and had a selfie taken, although he disappears in the actual picture (which is kind of creepy). Adherents are to praise him and pay tribute to his works (to persuade others to have their picture taken with him too). He wants all the credit for everything good and blames the creatures for everything bad (just as the creatures relate to him). In this pattern of relating, they need him all the more. The god beyond organized religion works through the creatures so the creatures get credit for the good and are held accountable for the bad (in their own interests). This god doesn't need to be the center of attention or a credit-grabber but finds satisfaction through indirect success. If this god seeks to "feel good" at all, it comes through the accomplishments of the creatures to create a more just society.

If there were no god, then we would have a tough time explaining why some creatures access energy to provide empathy while others remain narcissistic. Those who become empathic produce positive changes leading toward the resolution of conflict in their community peace-building efforts and work toward the redistribution of resources on an equitable scale.

---

15. Traditionally, the discussion regarding the existence of god does not ask what might be the god's interests in revealing himself.

Others continue to be emotional hoarders and fear that by sharing how they feel with others, they will lose a part of themselves. If everyone were empathic and didn't need to access energy to be so and if everyone worked to promote the interests of the common good, then we could conclude "there is no god." If this energy is produced by the human spirit and not the divine spirit, then we would have to explain why some have the capacity for empathy and others less so. We would not need a god if every human being was empathic (even though they are created to be so) and didn't need to develop critical thinking skills.

The practice of prayer and meditation seems to be one practice to access this energy. Praying to the god of organized religion is often to get him to change his mind so that he will do for us. In return, we are to be eternally grateful because our prayers were answered. The inverse would suggest that the energy flows the other way; that is it the god beyond organized religion who is trying to get us to change our mind so that we will do something to change the situation. The function of praying to the god beyond is to change the creature's mindset: to think things through to develop empathy and then to use that empathy to identify the most effective way to help another group of creatures. The target system of change is not the god, as if the god has made a mistake and the creatures are calling him on it, but to change the one reflecting and meditating.

Are There Multiple Gods?

Are there multiple gods each working for one of the major world religions and minor deities who work for the smaller companies, the ones not yet transported to another culture but remain native? Is there one god and each organization creates its own version, seemingly describing a detail of the big picture? What are the costs and benefits to a society when the belief in multiple gods is tolerated or even encouraged?

Organized religion functions under the following organizing principle regarding the gods: one god is affiliated with one religion and another god is affiliated with another religion. Global religions have become so divided within themselves, that it is unclear whether or not adherents of one denomination, movement or sect believe they are worshipping the same god. These divisions run emotionally deep for adherents. Supposedly, differences are doctrinal and political (and historical) and not theological, i.e., concept of god (one religion = one god). The assumption is that everyone

The God Beyond Organized Religion

within the same religious organization (representing one religion) worships the same god only divided by these technical differences. It is becoming increasing evident however that this is not the case. I have demonstrated that one's concept of god is developed with a variety of variables, from one's cultural environment to one's experiences and how one makes sense of those experiences.

If there is only one god and he works for one religion and not another, then we may infer that one religion worships the "true" god and everyone else worships a "fake" god. The problem with this deduction is that every religious organization, by virtue of being religious, perceives that it has the exclusive rights to the "one true god." (They may not publically denigrate the others for worshipping a counterfeit god but once I hear the word "truth," by implication those who worship another god do not worship a real god.) The ramifications from such thinking pour fuel on a passionate fire. I have already noted that it is not the different concepts that cause conflict among, between or within religious groups but the ways in which a society deals with difference and diversity. In other words, when society equips individuals to deal with culturally-derived differences (including religion), there is no need for one concept to compete with another for religious status or the god-of-the-year award.

In some societies, multiple gods live on the same land peacefully, coexisting quite amicably, even working together for the benefit of their constituents. In other societies, especially those associated with affluence and power, the native god (even if transported from elsewhere but no one remembers that historical journey) is associated with the dominant religion by which all newcomers are expected to worship or at least to pay tribute and honor. If the society's collective memory recalls that this god won the land (as a result of winning a war or decimating those already living on a particular plot of land) so that they could practice their religion upon it (a recurring theme), then everyone who subsequently immigrates to that land should worship that god. But when there is an influx of diverse cultural groups, naturally contributing to a process by which pluralism takes precedence over mono-optional choices (regarding concepts of god), the powerbrokers may becomes less tolerant and more insistent that everyone worship their god. They feel threatened that their god will have to compete with the new gods. Their thinking is, "When you are on our land, you have to worship our god."[16]

16. This group does not play well with others, especially when immigrants want

Reflections on the Search

Another option is that there is one god who has a closet full of designer clothes to dress for any occasion. When two religions depict god with different, even opposing, concepts, this merely reflects what the god chose to adorn this morning. Some days she wears stylish clothing and other days she wears frumpy fatigues. So when one religion claims they know god and this is what she is like, all they are doing is describing the outfit she chose to wear that day (and the outfit she wears may depend on what she has been summoned to do). If one religion is walking down the street and happens to see her, they assume that she wears that same outfit every day and unaware of the extent of her wardrobe (and perhaps she has a huge walk-in closet). Those who stand in a position of privilege tend to describe the part as if it represents the exclusive whole and can't comprehend why others are describing something different.[17]

Essentially, I have constructed a designer god rather than to subscribe a generic god (or purebred) who works for one particular religion, practiced by a particular organization (or an umbrella organization). I have granted myself creative license to pick and choose among the global religions in the process of conceiving this god. I have shopped at the specialty store, "build your own god." The smorgasbord of infinite possibilities serves to shape the spiritual stuffing. The images of god do not outfit its essence, but the functions, i.e., capacity to generate empathy, is what determines what to wear (and what not to wear). No longer are individuals beholden to the god of their family of origin or clan. Today, they seek avenues for experimentation to ascertain what makes sense for them. I realize that others may design a very different concept of god.

The god beyond organized religion requires some assembly. I prefer this method to prefabricated concepts that require no assembly and simply need someone to insert a triple-A battery so that it will work. We have become so systematized to having others do theological work for us that we feel incompetent to take on such an endeavor without proper training and grandiose leanings. Yes, there were times when one part didn't seem to fit with another, and frustration set in. But these could be times of learning

---

to keep the god they brought with them. Diversity is perceived as a threat to this royal claim rather than an opportunity to widen one's cultural lens to enhance one's own in the service of self-enlightenment.

17. It is often cited that each global religion is blindfolded and there is an elephant in the middle of the room. Each religion reaches out and touches it and then describes what they feel. They claim they know the elephant better than the others. But the elephant got tired of being poked and prodded and so returned to the herd.

The God Beyond Organized Religion

as we adapt to new challenges by changing the way we approach difficult subjects. We put things together in another way and when that worked we were quite pleased with ourselves. At other times, when all options were exhausted, we got out the saw and duck tape and made it fit a new way or just left that part off and made do. Now, I feel like the god is together as best as I can figure but one screw to complete the project is missing. Do I believe in the god beyond organized religion?[18] And if so, what would that belief look like in practice?

I don't think it is possible to tell whether the god worshipped by organized religion is the same god as the one beyond organized religion or if there are two (or more) gods. It may be that the one god can morph into different functions according to peon preference; that is, functions with whatever concept the peon wants or needs. During times when those who want the god just to perform some miracle, completely independent of all others, to swoosh down and remove the impending threat from the situation, are quite relieved to learn that there is a transactional god who is willing to do so. (I would have a problem with a god who only does this for those who believe in him however.) If this god is going to act that way, then it should do so based on the extent of need, the greatest suffering, to respond to the most desperate, and when he intervenes to have the biggest impact upon the most people. To exchange belief for individual whines, wishes and wants is counter to a theology of equality.

What distinguishes the two gods is the value of self-determination. Do we help others by doing for them or do we create environments that are more conducive to their being able to help themselves? While I can see that there are some situations in which we need to believe that there is a god who can reverse the current trauma or trend and perform a miracle because there would be nothing on earth we could do, there are clearly other situations in which we can do for ourselves. The god of organized religion provides fish, the god beyond teaches people how to fish and how

---

18. I also do not know if one has to believe in the god beyond to access this inspirational energy. Self and other awareness is usually a good thing when it comes to helping other people to help themselves but I do not doubt that occasionally someone inadvertently also does something significant. Believing that we have such energy (whether we believe its source is divine or human) is probably the most important of all beliefs. The disconnection seems to arise when people say, "I know here are poor people and I want to help. I just don't know what to do." This is where empathy and critical thinking skills mixed together (and I have made the argument one without the other dilutes the potential for effective intervention) come into play. We need to believe in ourselves so that we can access the potential for changing the world in which we live.

to preserve their coral reefs so that they can produce another generation of big fish to feed another generation of people. Our methods of intervention to alleviate poverty, reduce the effects of global warming and work toward advocating for equality for all are dependent upon our conceptualizing a god who models transformative intervention.

In Reflection

At this lookout in our spiritual journey, I would like to offer a few apologetic comments to those who worship the god of organized religion. I mean no disrespect toward those who have found comfort and solace in believing in a transactional god. Some of my best friends are religious. I take full responsibility for making some seemingly critical comments concerning the concept of the god they worship. My intent is not to prove them wrong nor imply that their faith is false or their god is a fake. I am impressed with the strength of their convictions, even if I do not share them. I too have invested much energy in thinking about the god of organized religion, so much so that he might even assume that this is a book about him, like he walked into the party as if he was walking onto a yacht. I would not want to suggest that the god of organized religion does not exist.

Indeed, what I am challenging is the way in which we relate to a god, the god or any god for that matter. I am confronting the notion that god needs us to do something to invoke or respond to divine intervention, affection or expression. I can no longer believe that my best friend did something to instigate his wrath or failed to be religious enough so as to deserve a divine miracle which would have saved her. I can no longer believe that god loves some people more than others, explaining why some people are poor, oppressed or marginalized. It doesn't make sense. Still, it is quite possible, in my thinking, that the god of organized religion exists and doesn't want people to think that about him but can't get the religious organizers to shut up about their perception of his transactional nature. They would be out of jobs (not the gods) if they were not needed because people could talk to god on their own and could directly access divine energy to be more empathic.

It may be, then, that it is our concept of god in need of change and not the god. Perhaps we have insisted that the god of organized religion accept the adaptive challenge to be less transactional and more transformative and in reality, it is us who need to shift the way we relate to each other

The God Beyond Organized Religion

(reflected in the way we relate to god). A way to make this transition would be to change our concept of god from being transactional to transformative. By making this change, people would begin to do for others without expecting anything in return (just as the god does not expect anything in return). Repeated behaviors eventually change perception and attitude and those who go about helping others would become more empathic toward their circumstance which, in turn, would inspire them to want to help even more (and to offer more effective help).[19] Instead of waiting for god to be the kind of god we need why don't we go out and be the kind of person that god needs us to be.

I know she has been with me throughout the writing of this book. I have felt her presence, heard her laughter and been inspired by her encouragement. At every step in the process, I was aware our conversations about god which continued even after she died and went to heaven. I felt her spirit with me just as powerfully as I did when she was among the living. Only because I have gone through this experience, has it been possible for me to arrive at a different place in my thinking about a god beyond organized religion. I did not make this journey alone. Still, I miss her every day. At night, when I look up to the heavens, I sing to her, don't you know that you are a shooting star?

---

19. I have attempted to demonstrate, throughout this discourse, that there is a difference in helping people with the formation of empathy, because empathy improves critical thinking skills. Helping people, preserving the planet, protecting the rights of the oppressed, cannot be a totally rational course. If the god beyond showed up tomorrow and took some food from the rich and redistributed it to the poor, the rich would not be changed. (They might just be pissed off.) To teach people how to actively listen to each other so that they improve their patterns of relating, that is preferable than to tie them to a chair and command, "Listen and for god's sake, look interested." There is a difference in the nature of the help from someone who is doing it because it is helping them to resolve the tension between their selfish and selfless selves and those who are helping for purely or close to purely selfish reasons (e.g., to avoid a consequence or receive a reward).

www.ingramcontent.com/pod-product-compliance
Lightning Source LLC
Chambersburg PA
CBHW071508150426
43191CB00009B/1451